745.5
G 882i
DISCARDED
JENKS LRC
GORDON COLLEGE

AN INTRODUCTION TO BASIC CRAFTS

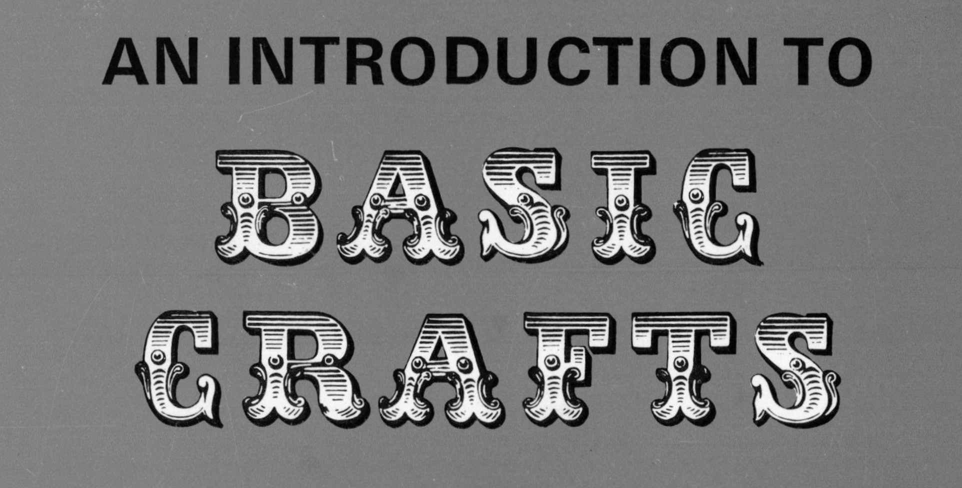

GRETCHEN GRIMM

James Wozniak, potter.

AN INTRODUCTION TO

by

GRETCHEN GRIMM, B.S.,M. Ed.

Associate Professor of Art
Wisconsin State University
Eau Claire, Wisconsin

Burgess Publishing Company

426 South Sixth Street • Minneapolis, Minn. 55415

Burgess

EDUCATION SERIES

Consulting Editor — LAURENCE S. FLAUM

COOPERATION FOR BETTER STUDENT TEACHING . . . . Bennie

GUIDANCE A LONGITUDINAL APPROACH . . . . Blanchard-Flaum

CREDO FOR AMERICAN PUBLIC EDUCATION . . . . Flaum

EFFECTIVE SECONDARY EDUCATION . . . . Lueck, et. al.

TECHNIQUES FOR TEACHING CONSERVATION EDUCATION . . . . Brown-Mouser

THE BEGINNING KINDERGARTEN TEACHER . . . . . Salot-Leavitt

INTEGRATING OUTDOOR AND CONSERVATION EDUCATION INTO THE CURRICULUM . . . . Stapp

INVESTIGATIONS IN PHYSICAL SCIENCE . . . . Strickland

RESEARCH FOR TEACHERS AND COUNSELORS . . . . Tolbert

PHOTOSITUATIONS: A TECHNIQUE FOR TEACHING . . . . Potter-Moss-Smith

---

Printed in the United States of America

Library of Congress Catalog Card Number 68-15376

Second Printing 1969

FOREWORD

The crafts have been with us for a long time. The man-made object as shaped by craftsmen has given us the record of mankind from prehistoric times through the present era. Even with the advent of almost total mechanization the creative and imaginative capacities of the sincere craftsman stand forth. The products of his craft are cherished and bring a fine sense of beauty for the beholder. The men and women who have given us these products have held contact with tradition. They have attended to the requirements of process and materials; but they have also, through the exercise of judgment, broken from conformity to think originally and to create work in which their own personal qualities come through. Usually the craftsman works with the oldest and simplest of tools and directs all of the work himself, from design through execution. Like his predecessor, the contemporary craftsman uses ancient processes, refines them and makes such applications that are consistent with ideas and thinking of the modern world. Many traditional craft processes have been revived. The artist does not hide from history, but with flexibility and imagination has directed these processes to a higher level of individuality. Although for a long time we have made rather arbitrary decisions about what would be called a craft and what should be called a fine art, we are now aware of the fact that the craftsman becomes an artist when the things he makes expresses or excites feeling.

We live at a time when outrageous claims are made about the products of commerce and industry—–for soap, household appliances, and cosmetics. Often the value of publications is exaggerated. It is refreshing to read a book by an author who states at the beginning precisely what is intended and then proceeds to accomplish these things.

The author of *An Introduction to Basic Crafts* is an experienced teacher. She understands and appreciates the needs and aspirations of the novice or the beginning student. This book has been designed for the people who believe that "art is for all of us". Each of the crafts that have been selected is treated with precision and clarity; the step by step directions are explained and reinforced by the excellent photographs that bring the reader close to a craftsman at work. This book is for the beginner, the child or adult who will teach himself or will be taught by others. Its applications are many; it can be used by people at home and at school and in recreation centers or camps who have the strong desire to make objects that are both beautiful and useful. Throughout the text the author has conveyed the idea that these crafts—–the earliest of our art forms—–have a new dignity that expresses our time and our culture.

Reid Hastie
Professor of Art Education
University of Minnesota

ACKNOWLEDGMENTS

Many years and many minds have gone into this publication. One author could not create this text alone. Credit should be given to many. First, I wish to thank my students and friends who cooperated whole-heartedly. Regretfully, they are too numerous to name.

I am especially indebted to the following: Dr. Reid Hastie for his Foreword; Judy Carlson for her patience and perfectionism in helping me; Edmund Lewandowski for his photographs of the War Memorial Facade; James Wozniak for his photographs of ceramics; Robert Benton for his editing and Dr. Vernon Gingerich for proof reading of the manuscript; and last, but by no means least, all who produced samples for photographs, participated in photographs, and believed in this publication.

One of the greatest attributes of this book is its photographs. Most of these were taken and developed by Susan O'Neil in the photography laboratory at Wisconsin State University at Eau Claire under the direction of Mr. Richard Beckman. My sincere appreciation to Mrs. O'Neil. Credit is given for the photographs of the War Memorial Building in Milwaukee to the Milwaukee *Journal*. Photographs of James Wozniak are by Steve Alexander of Fort Worth, Texas. The photograph of the Minneapolis, Minnesota, Aquatennial Float is from Minnesota Mining and was executed by Dayton's of Minneapolis. Photographs for the Chapter on Plastics were taken and developed by James Christopherson, Wisconsin State University, Eau Claire, Wisconsin.

G. G.
January 1968

SPECIAL ACKNOWLEDGMENTS

Chapter V
Herb Brodt, BS, MA
Public Schools, Chetek, Wisconsin

Chapter VIII
Judith B. Carlson, BS
Stout State University, Menomonie, Wisconsin

Chapter IX
Robb Wilson, BFA, MA, MFA
Stout State University, Menomonie, Wisconsin

Photo Illustrations by
Susan O'Neil and others

DEDICATION

Not to the ivory tower, nor the sophisticates, nor the long-haired men, but to the grass roots people who believe art is for ALL people, this book is respectfully dedicated.

CONTENTS

GENERAL INTRODUCTION

This book is just what its title states: *An Introduction to Basic Crafts.* It is written for the novice. These chapters present ten basic crafts. One may begin with his favorite craft and work from the simple to the complex. Although the basic steps for each procedure are given, a creative approach is maintained.

If at times, while reading and working with this book, you find that some directions are not as complete as you would like, you may know that it has been our intent to encourage individual expression. We hope you will express yourself without dictation. Where direction ends, creative imagination must take over. This is the point where one's craft becomes a creative activity.

Civilizations the world over have been involved with constructive activities and pastimes for both aesthetic and practical pleasure. All people have enriched their culture by participating in the crafts. Crafts, as linked to the past, present a reflection of the history of man and his culture. Man has always used his hands. In every period of history in every land man has worked with crafts – clay, leather, metal, and others – sometimes as a necessity, but always as an outlet. Wood and stone were first shelters for survival; equally utilitarian were the tools men created. Soon man was not satisfied with shelter to keep out the wind and rain. He sought ornamentation to satisfy his aesthetic longings.

From earliest times, man has used the hides and skins of animals for his benefit. Leather was developed very early and used not only for clothing and shelter but for decorative purposes as well. In the thirteenth century Marco Polo found soft leather bed coverlets used in India. During the Middle Ages, craft guilds produced high quality workmanship in the making of short leather breeches and other wearing apparel. The American Indians learned that by wearing leather moccasins they could run faster over rough ground and pursue game without hurting their feet. For the early American colonist, leather was an indispensible item for shoes, breeches, belts, jackets, saddles, and saddlebags.

The craft of copper enameling dates back thousands of years. Definite evidence proves its use in 80 B.C.

Mosaics were common during the Byzantine and Early Christian periods.

Pottery was an obvious necessity at first. Today it is highly aesthetic and decorative, as well as practical.

The history and development of crafts may be traced, but it is the present and the future with which this book is concerned. The above historical information simply indicates the deep roots of all crafts. Today we use craft materials and experiences to create articles for *our* time and to use the materials of *our* culture.

Many books have been and shall be written on the crafts: their backgrounds, their offerings, and their possibilities. Some discuss several fields; others only one. In some cases hundreds of books have been written on one single craft. (Note the bibliography of this book.) Yet, all this writing deals not with words so much as with feelings, emotions, and experiences. To write about crafts is difficult. What can one person write which will inspire and direct others: How can one write or talk about something which is so intangible and indescribable?

Any one of the crafts included in this book is a challenging field of study in itself. For example, the study of *ceramics* is a profession. It can be a lifetime study and has been for untold persons. The profession of the potter, as a commercial venture or as an aesthetic endeavor, is not unusual. Increasing numbers of people are engaged in this craft as commercial potters, teachers, students of ceramics, and hobbyists. This is a field which has been and will be popular for its offering of practical vessels, its aesthetic challenge to artists of every age and ability, and its function as a hobby and an emotional outlet for the novice of seven to seventy years.

The field of crafts is available to *all*, not just to the "talented few." It is not only a fascinating and constructive leisure time activity, but it may be helpful in giving release to pent up emotions and energies and in granting rewarding visual results which can be both aesthetic and profitable. It may be an activity for individual expression and pleasure, or it may be a group project which develops "give and take" and creates a sense of cooperation and democracy.

The field of crafts may be as basic and homespun as grandma's braided rugs or as sophisticated and complicated as tomorrow's design. There is something for everyone. Projects may range from those without cost to those which are extremely expensive.

Some crafts require complete directions while others are so suggestive that creativity is a necessity. Whatever the simplicity or sophistication, whatever the needs or desires, one will find suggestions for constructive leisure, individual and group participation, and many hours of happiness in these truly rewarding and creative experiences.

This work is limited in its choice of crafts. There are many, and each, in turn, deserves its place in the sun. Through the years certain crafts, like great cultures, have risen and fallen, become popular and then faded into oblivion. The crafts in this book were not chosen because they were the best or the greatest or the most popular. They are the ones I have recently enjoyed, and I want to share this enjoyment with you.

Whatever the craft, remember that the intent of this book is purely to introduce. A number of projects, from the simple to the complex, will be presented in relation to each craft. If the stimulation is great enough, you may pursue further the craft of your choice. Three avenues are open to you—that of the commercial producer, the aesthetic research artist, or the happy hobbyist.

Despite all the years in which "education" has tried to lead the way to stimulate great minds, it has continually failed to accept the endeavors and merits of the creative fields of study; art, music, drama, and dance. Education has been basically concerned with the three R's. In this world where education is too often geared to the acquiring of knowledge, creative activities should play a complementary role. Science and other specialized fields have improved material standards of living, but they have done little to aid creative life needs. *An Introduction to Basic Crafts* is intended to stimulate creative activities and to give pleasure and enrichment.

Edmund Lewandowski's Mosaic War Memorial, Milwaukee, Wisconsin.

Materials needed:
Cloth
Dye, ink, or paint (water, oil, or textile paint)
Simple articles appropriate to each project
- wax crayons
- string
- frames
- stencil paper
- cutting tools
- wood
- linoleum
- silk
- squeegees
- mucilage
- tusche
- paint for silk screen
- brushes
- turpentine
- wax

APPLICATION OF DESIGN TO FABRICS

One of the most practical arts is that of decorating fabrics. Drapes, bed spreads, table cloths, place mats, handkerchiefs, scarves, napkins, ties, shirts, skirt lengths, and other articles of clothing can be personalized and enriched by the use of applied design. Materials ranging from fine silks and satins to the extreme rough texture of burlap are usable. The processes vary, like all other crafts, from the very simple to the most complex.

Ancient civilizations the world over have found great satisfaction and a means to display their culture by producing beautiful hand-designed tapestries, rugs, and other articles created out of fabrics. For example, ancient oriental batik is one of the finest samples of a genuine craft that our history has ever known.

A few basic steps are common to all types of fabric design.

1. All cloth should be washed before application of a design to remove the sizing and filler. Use warm, soapy water and rinse thoroughly.
2. All cloth should be ironed to remove wrinkles.
3. Preplanning and designing should be done on paper before attempting applications of any kind of cloth. The design should be planned carefully with the cloth, the technique, and the use of the fabric well in mind.
4. A suitable cloth as well as suitable paint or dye should be selected for each process.
5. Colors are usually set with 350° F. ironing applied over cloth protection for one minute. Turn and repeat.

Figure 1. Original silk screen drape made by Robbie Gund

PROJECT 1: TIE DYE HANDKERCHIEF
(Figure 2)

1. Choose cloth which is not too stiff or coarse. Silk, rayon, or cotton is good. A plain white handkerchief will serve. Wash the fabric to remove sizing. After it is washed and ironed, tie the cloth with string, as in *Figure 3*. The more surface that is tied with string the more cloth will remain white because the string will serve as a repellent against the dye. The usual design is obtained by pulling each corner out, tying thoroughly in several places, and then pulling out the exact center and tying. Vary the distance between the tied sections to make the dyed pattern more interesting.
2. When all tying has been completed, place the cloth in dye according to the directions given with the dye.
3. Remove from the dye and dry.
4. Carefully cut and unwrap the cords to remove from the cloth.
5. Press.

More than one color may be used by dying the lighter color first, wrapping cord around parts of it that are to show up in the finished cloth, and then dying the remaining cloth a darker color. Overlap of color sometimes proves extremely interesting.

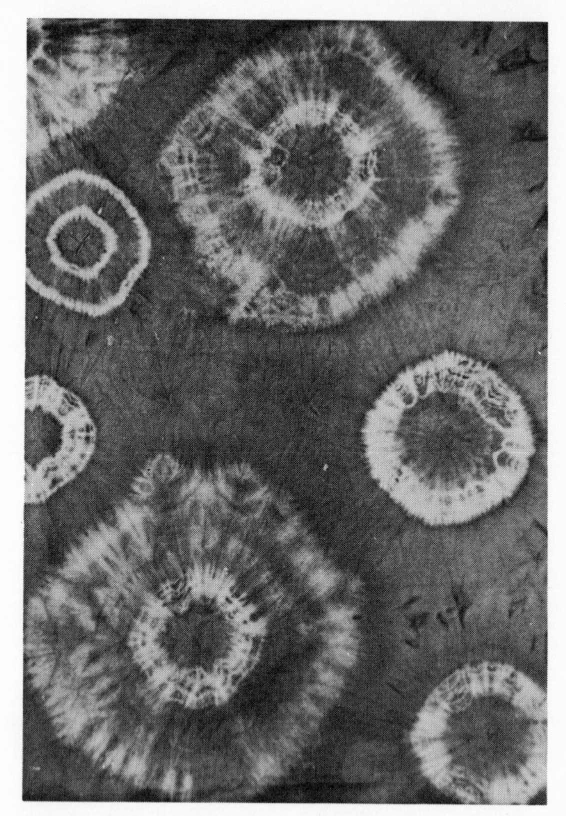

Figure 2. Tie dye

Figure 3. Tie cloth

Figure 4. Crayon stencil

Figure 5. Stencil and print

PROJECT 2: CRAYON PLACE MATS
(Figure 4)

1. A suggested material for place mats, one which takes crayon color well and is inexpensive, is unbleached muslin. Butcher linen, burlap, and similar materials are also good. Cut cloth to size, about 12" x 18". If a hem is to be put in, allow in size for it. If fringe is used, additional size must be allowed – 14" x 22" total. Pinking shears may be used.
2. On a piece of paper, the same size as the place mats, plan your design. Simple motifs such as leaves, initials, nature motifs, flowers, butterflies, fish, and birds are good. These may be applied to the space in the border, all over, or singularly.
3. Transfer the design by tracing it onto the cloth with graphite paper. This gives a tracing but does not leave a strong black greasy line as does regular carbon. If you can make free hand designs without tracing, it is better. You also can stencil on design as in *Figure 5.*
4. Color the design with crayon directly onto the cloth. Press firmly and work the crayon color into the fabric. *(Figure 6)*
5. Place newspaper on the ironing board and iron, as in *Figure 7*, or put cloth on the ironing board upside down. Place papers on top of the cloth and iron with a hot iron. Crayon wax colors will steam and melt into the cloth and will be permanent for washing.

Figure 6. Color stencil

Figure 7. Iron cloth

PROJECT 3: SIMPLE PRINT PROCESSES PLACE MAT OR WALL HANGING

(Figure 8)

1. On paper try printing with simple print materials, such as a sponge, a spool, a fork, a chore boy, a half cabbage. *(Figure 9)* Put tempera paint of the desired color on a plate, a glass, or a flat non-absorbent surface. With a spoon or spatula rub the paint around the plate into an area about 6" in diameter. This smear of paint should be thin. Dip a sponge, spool, chore boy, half of cabbage, or anything interesting in shape (even a cookie cutter) into this paint. Press it on the paper. Repeat. Try singles, all over patterns, or border repeats. A sponge or stamp pad may also be used for printing. Try to print with many articles of your home or school, even those which are in your junk box. Vegetables, like the half cabbage, a cut carrot, or a half potato cut into a design, form nice prints.
2. Print some of these on paper or cloth (singularly, border, or all over). For cloth you must use an oil base paint, such as oil paint, oil printer's ink, or any good textile paint. Follow the rules of regular textile painting – washing the cloth first and preparing the appropriate cloth for the special project. If you choose to use textile paint, follow the directions given for this paint.
3. Finish by ironing carefully.

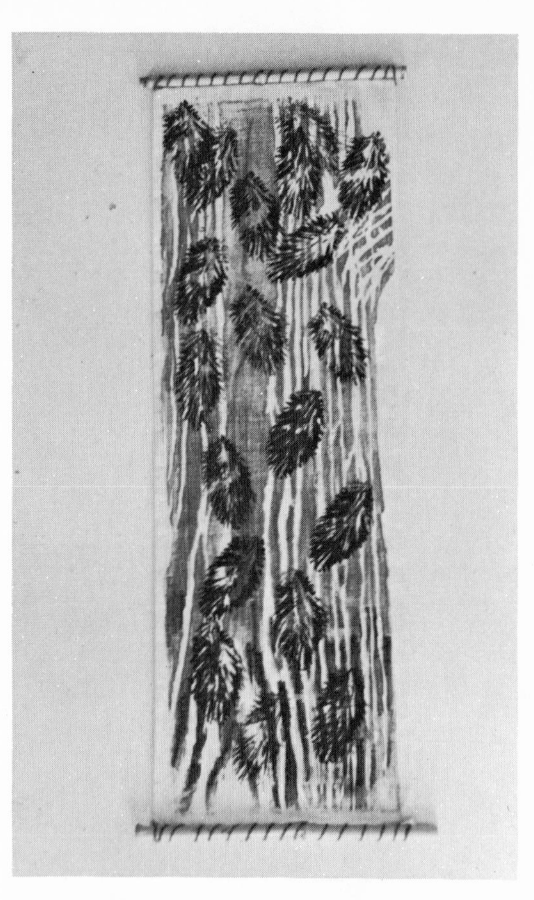

Figure 8. Printed wall hanging

Figure 9. Gadget printing

PROJECT 4: STENCIL TABLE CLOTH

(Figure 10)

The process of stenciling involves the covering and exposure of parts of your design; all parts covered remain untouched by color and will be the original color of the cloth. All parts cut away in the stencil receive the color and form the design.

1. Cloth for a table should be appropriate for your needs concerning durability, occasion for use, and endurance in water.
2. Prepare the cloth by washing out the sizing and by ironing.
3. On paper prepare your design. Practice the stencil process. The stencil process is executed in the following manner: in designs, you may use either a "negative" or "positive" stencil. For example, you may draw a form on paper or cut a free hand shape (realistic or imaginary in shape). Note the two cut outs in *Figure 11.* One is a positive impression, the other negative. Either or both could be used as a stencil.
4. After practice with ordinary paper, draw your design on a stiff grade paper or stencil paper. Stencil paper is slightly waxed and stiff and, therefore, better for this work. Cut the design from stencil paper with scissors, razor, or a sharp knife.
5. Fasten the stencil to the cloth. The washed and ironed cloth is better when stretched over soft wood and tacked or taped to the wood with masking tape. The stencil may then be pinned securely in place.
6. Apply color by the stiff brush method shown in *Figure 12,* the tooth brush method in *Figure 13,* or the new commercial spray can method in *Figure 14.* Your stencil will be more successful if you remember the following:
   a. Fasten the stencil securely to keep the design clear cut.
   b. Color should be heaviest around the outside edges and lightest in the center part of the cut outs.
   c. More than one color may be used, even in one area, and will prove interesting. In other words, blending of colors is best done directly on the cloth.
   d. Be sure to work colors well into the fabric for this accounts for half of their retention value.
7. Allow the color to dry thoroughly.
8. When the color is thoroughly dry, remove the pins and carefully remove the stencil. Your stenciled table cloth is now ready to hem and iron.

Figure 10. Stenciled tablecloth

STENCIL TECHNIQUES

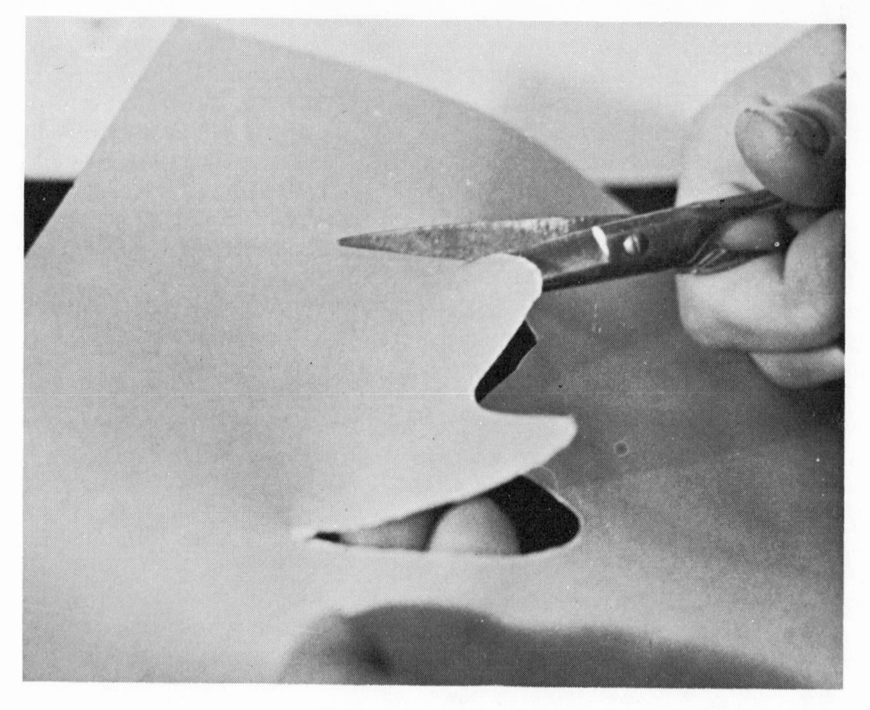

Figure 11. Cut stencil

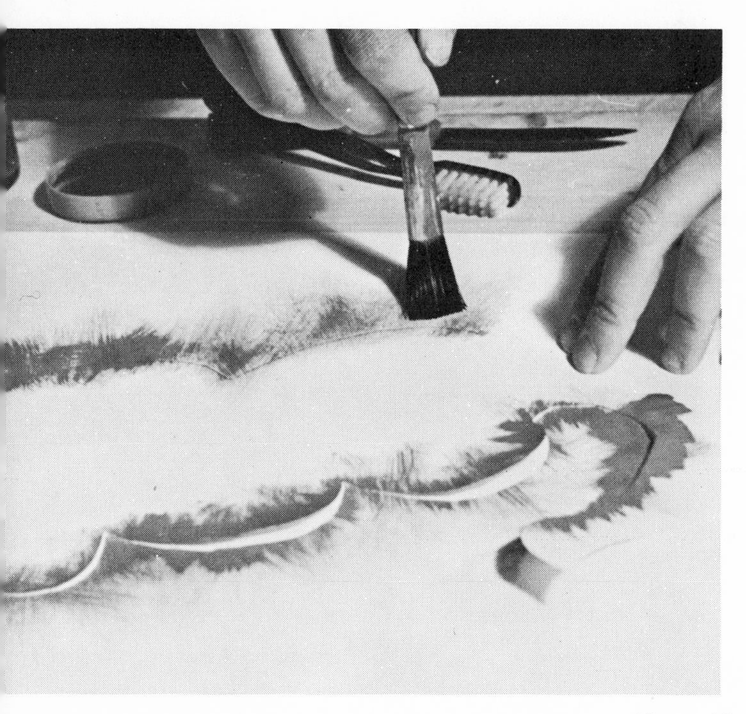

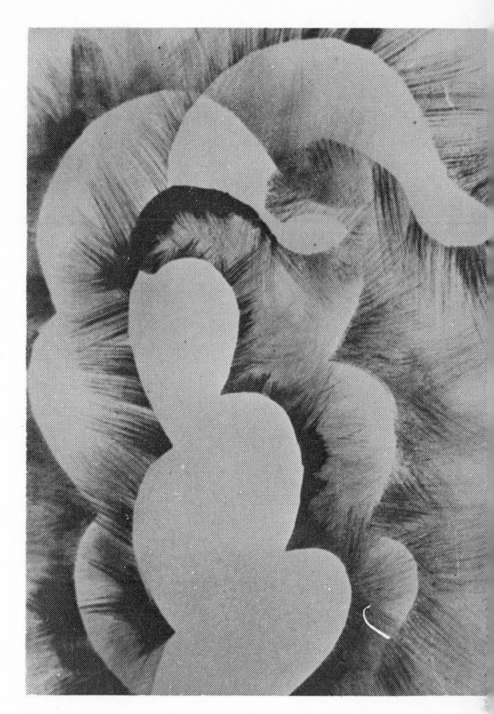

Figure 12. Brush stencil

Figure 13. Toothbrush stencil

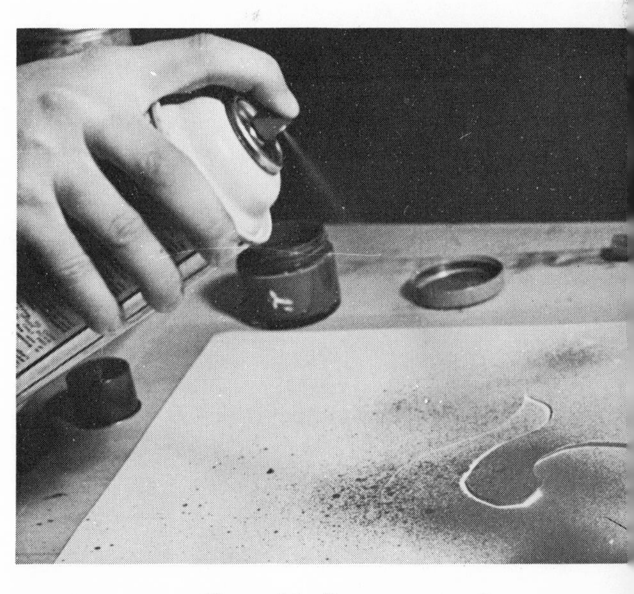

Figure 14. Spray can stencil

PROJECT 5: BLOCK PRINT CLOTH
(Figure 15)

The block print denotes a print from cut linoleum or wood. From a piece of linoleum or soft wood, part is cut away and part is left. The part that remains receives the color and stamps the print. This process is basically similar to the rubber stamp or the printing press.

1. Draw a design of your choice on practice paper. When you have achieved the design you want, transfer it backwards to your piece of wood or linoleum. Usually designs are worked out in only black and white, one representing the part to be left and the other the part that is to be cut away.
2. With a gouging tool, cut part away and leave part. *Figure 16* shows a linoleum block and *Figure 17* shows wood. Remember, everything you cut away will remain the color of the cloth or original paper; everything left standing will catch the ink and print the color. In wood, cut *with* the grain and use the grain for part of your design. Be sure to keep your non-cutting hand back or at the side of the tool. Parts that are cut away need not be clean-cut (especially in the wood cut) because the effect of the remaining grain is interesting.
3. When the block is cut, it is ready to be printed. Processes of applying the print vary from such simple processes as daubing on paint, placing the block on cloth, and applying pressure, to that as complicated as the mechanical printing presses. One suggested process which anyone may do simply and without machinery follows:
   a. Place the cloth flat on many level layers of newspaper.
   b. Squeeze ink from printer's ink tube onto glass. *(Figure 18)*
   c. Roll a brayer over the ink a number of times *(Figure 19)* until it becomes "tacky."
   d. Roll the inked brayer over the block (both ways), thoroughly covering the parts not cut away. *(Figure 20)*
   e. Place the inked block on cloth or paper.
   f. Apply pressure by standing on the block. tapping it with a hammer, or rubbing it with a spoon. *(Figure 21)*
   g. Remove the block, the print is made. *(Figure 22)*
   h. Repeat as the design requires.
4. After the block has been printed the number of times desired, let the cloth dry and press for use.

Figure 15. Block print

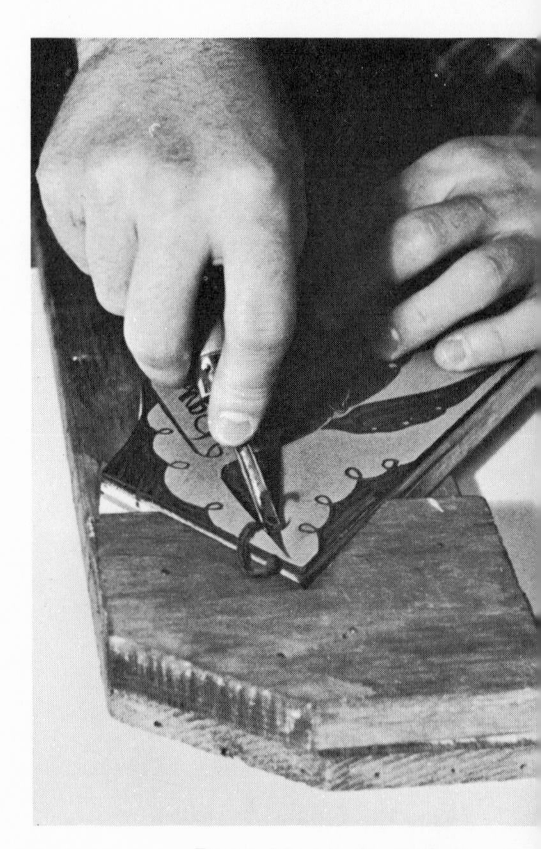

Figure 16. Linoleum block

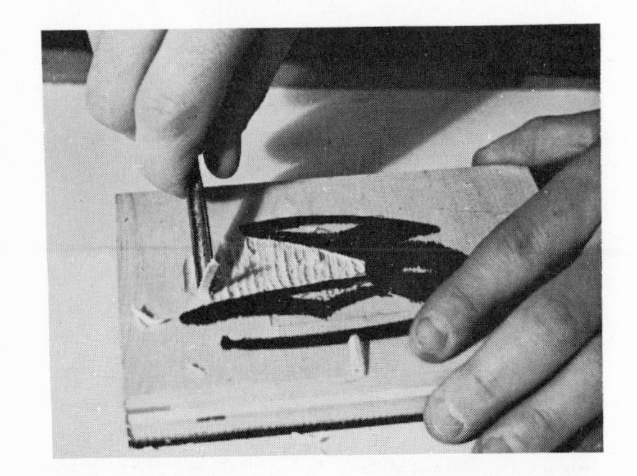

Figure 17. Wood block

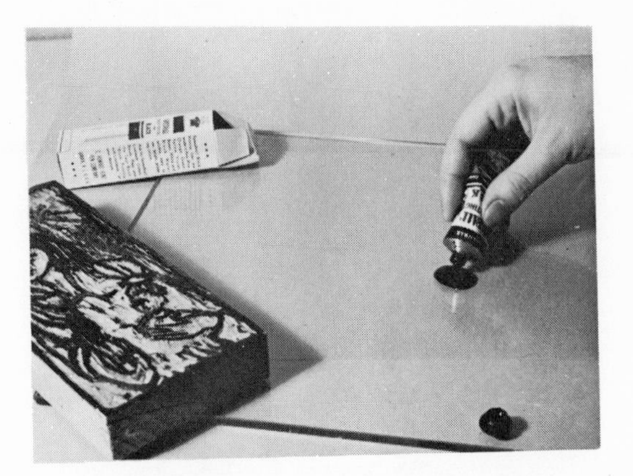

Figure 18. Squeeze printer's ink on glass

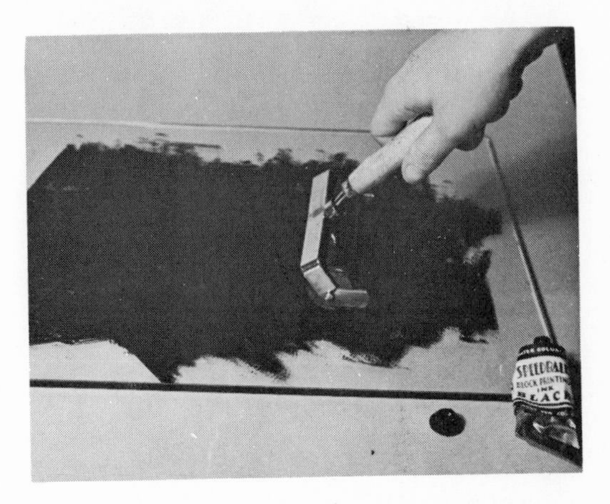

Figure 19. Roll brayer over the ink

Figure 20. Roll inked brayer over the block

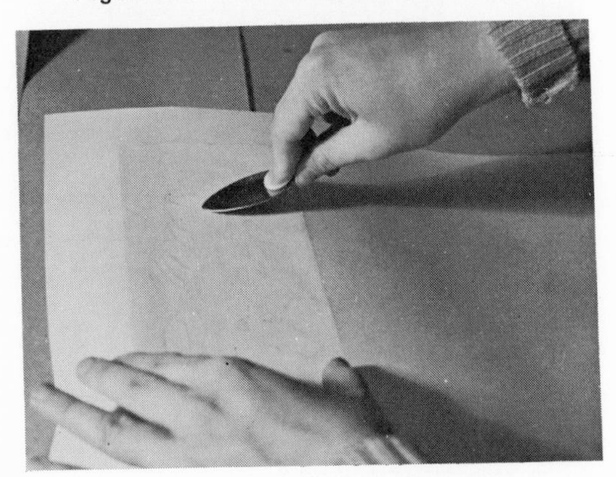

Figure 21. Apply pressure

Figure 22. A woodcut and print

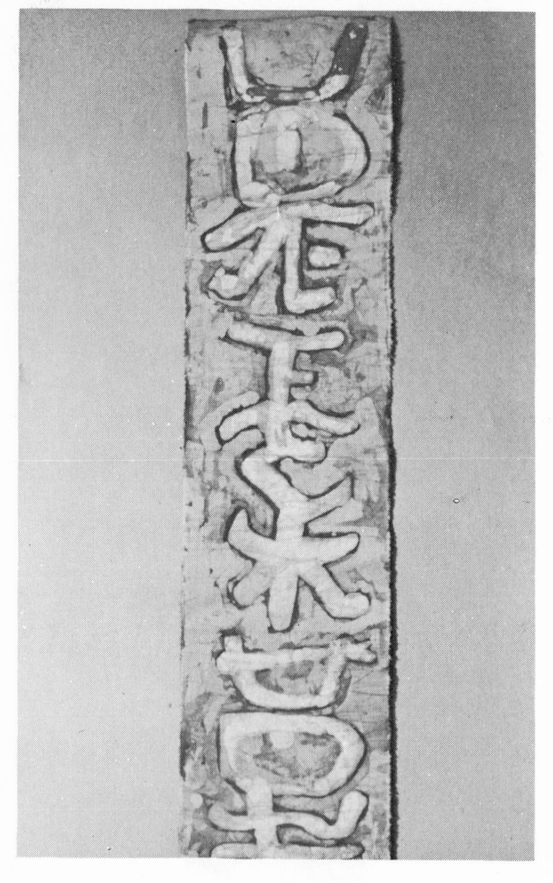

Figure 23. Batik

PROJECT 6: BATIK *(Figure 23)*

The batik process involves wax resistant to dye. It is a beautiful old technique which originated in the Orient. Cloth for batik should be fairly light weight such as silk, rayon, chiffon, or light weight percale.

1. Draw a design the size desired.
2. Prepare the cloth for wax by washing and ironing it. Square the cloth and stretch it on a wooden frame. Lay the paper design underneath. The light silk will allow you to see through to the design.
3. Melt the wax (para-wax or beeswax) over low heat. A coffee can is a good container for melting the wax. When the wax is melted, it is ready to be painted on the cloth. *(Figure 24)* Paint with wax all the area which you wish to retain in the original color of the cloth. A brush (No. 7) works well to give thin lines and also to fill in larger areas.
4. When the wax is applied and dry, remove the cloth from the frame. Dip it into the dye and follow the directions on the dye package. Almost any good commercial dye may be used. Some of the wax may crack, and the dye will run into these cracks. This is typical of batik and furnishes interesting patterns.
5. When the dye is dry, the wax is removed by placing the cloth between layers of paper on the ironing board and ironing with a very hot iron. Change papers. Repeat. Wax may also be removed by dipping cloth into a cleaning fluid. The piece may be finished or you may repeat the process, waxing other parts and dying with another color. Where a several-color process is desired, first dye the lightest color and proceed to darker colors. Batik is especially suited to wall hangings, drapes, place mats, and scarves.

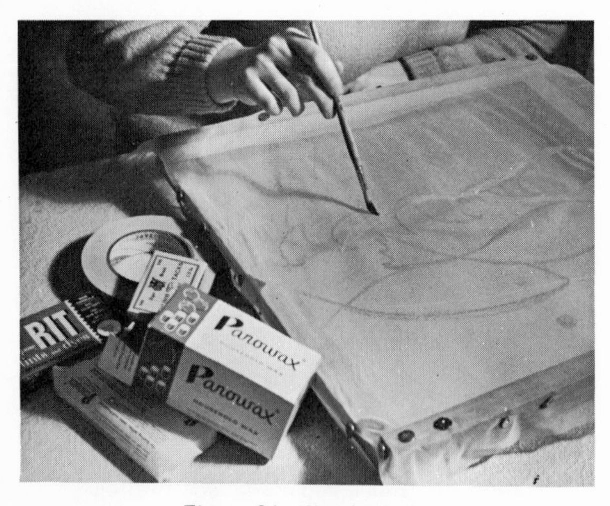

Figure 24. Wax in design

Finished Batik

Figure 25. Silk screen series

PROJECT 7: SILK SCREEN *(Figure 25)*

The silk screen is our own modern interpretation and expression of what is probably the oldest type of printing process. It is a stencil process. Again, we can thank the Orient for this art. The process of silk screening has many possibilities. (For further study see the listing of books on other processes of silk screening.) For a simple explanation of the tusche and glue process, follow the illustrated steps:

1. Draw an original design. *(Figure 26)*
2. Prepare the screen for printing. *(Figure 27)* Screens may be purchased or made. If you make your own use white pine lumber 1" x 2", kiln dried and free from knots. About five lineal feet are needed for an individual frame 12" x 18". The frame must be rigid to support the tightly stretched cloth and the paint. Miter joints may be made and fastened with cleats. Reinforce the corners with angle irons on the side or with "L" irons on top. Cut a piece of silk, nylon, dacron or organdy somewhat larger than the frame and stretch this tightly over the frame. Tack the silk at one corner of the frame. Stretch it along one of the short sides and tack it. At the opposite end of the frame, pull the silk tight in the center. Tack the center being sure the weave of the silk is parallel to the sides of the frame. Pull and tack entire end. Tack the two other sides. To further protect the tacked edges, the surface of the frame is taped. Use a glue-solution of one part glue and three parts water to moisten the gummed tape. Tape frame overlapping ¼ of an inch to ½ inch of the silk mesh. Apply a coat of shellac to all the taped areas inside and out.

Attach this frame with loose pin butt hinges to the base. Any flat wood surface which is larger than the frame will be satisfactory. A drawing board may be used. In some cases the frame is attached directly to the table top. Strips of tape may be placed on the base to serve as register guides.

Attach a drop stick about 10" to 12" long to the side of the frame. It should be attached in such a manner that it swings loosely and will drop into position when the frame is raised. This drop stick serves to keep the screen frame away from the printing surface while a fresh piece of printing stock is being inserted.

3. Put the screen over the design. *(Figure 28)*
4. When the screen is over the design you are able to see through the screen to the design. Cover the design with tusche. *(Figure 29)* (Tusche is the commercial name for the black-out ink; it may be obtained at most craft stores.)
5. When the design is painted onto the silk with tusche, lift the frame and remove your original design. *(Figure 30)* Allow tusche about one half hour to dry.
6. Place the screen on the prop. *(Figure 31)*
7. Paint liquid glue on the screen to cover all parts around the design. *(Figure 32)* Hold the screen to the light to make sure all areas are covered with glue. Dry glue thoroughly.
8. Remove the tusche after the glue is dried. Turpentine or kerosene dissolves the tusche but does not effect the dried glue. *(Figure 33)* Wipe the screen with a cloth saturated with turpentine or kerosene, then wipe with a clean dry cloth until it is thoroughly dry.
9. The screen is now ready for print. *(Figure 34)*
10. Place a clean paper under the screen. Apply silk screen paint ready to print. *(Figure 35)*
11. Pull the paint across the design with a squeegee. *(Figure 36)* A squeegee is a rubber blade sandwiched into a wooden housing.
12. When you pull the paint entirely across the screen you have covered your design completely with paint. *(Figure 37)*
13. Raise the screen frame. The print should be an exact copy of the original. *(Figure 38)*

Figure 26. Draw original design

Figure 27. Prepare the screen

Figure 28. Put screen over the design

Figure 29. Cover the design with tusche

Figure 32. Paint on liquid glue

Figure 30. Remove the original design

Figure 31. Place the screen on the prop

Figure 33. Dissolve tusche

Figure 34. Screen ready to print

Figure 37. Screen covered with paint

Figure 35. Apply silk screen paint

Figure 38. Printed paper

Figure 36. Pull paint across with squeegee

BASKETRY AND RAFFIA

Materials needed:

Basics
- reed or raffia for spokes
- weavers (thinner reed)
- a base (usually plywood—crate wood is fine)
- glue
- sandpaper
- shellac
- water and container

Extras
- insets for planters or vases

Reed has been used throughout the years because it has been easily available. It has been used for everything from baskets to beds, boats to bridges. Reed is basically a growth of nature. When soaked in water, it is pliable and can be formed into any shape – bent and woven into baskets, planters, trays. Today, we do not turn to nature for this material, though we easily could. It is now available in craft stores. Kits for making baskets and other forms are also available. It is more interesting, however, to take a more creative approach; buy your reed by the pound, and design and plan your own projects.

Use a base of wood, preferably ¼" plywood. In all reed work there must be an uneven number of spokes in the base to make the weaving possible. All reed must be thoroughly soaked in water at least ½ hour before work is begun and during the process of weaving. Dry reed will crack and break and is not pliable for weaving and shaping.

Figure 1
Wisconsin Indian hand-made basket

PROJECT 1: SMALL ROUND REED BASKET *(Figure 2)*

1. Take a round piece of crate or ¼" plywood 4" in diameter. *(Figure 3)* Drill an uneven number of holes 1/8" in diameter around the outside edge about ¼" in from the edge. There should be about 13 holes, evenly spaced. *(Figure 4)*
2. Use 13 pieces of reed for the spokes, 10" long. Soak them in water. *(Figure 5)* At the same time soak the thinner weaver raffia. Allow these to soak about ½ hour. Spokes and weavers must be kept moist while working with them.
3. Push the spokes through the holes in the base. Let them extend about 2" on the underneath side. *(Figure 6)*
4. Weave the spokes around the bottom to seal off securely. Begin with number 1 spoke. Weave the 2" lower part around the outside of number 2 spoke and lock it in front of number 3. Weave the number 2 spoke around number 3 and lock it in front of number 4, and so on. Continue this until all are locked. Press the woven spokes firmly against the bottom of the base. *(Figure 7)*
5. Weave the top. Bend the wet spokes slightly outward above the base so the sides of the basket will slant out. Continue to do this occasionally as you weave the basket. Take a length of thin weaver reed about 15' long. Weave this thin reed in and out around the spokes, making sure the ends of starting and ending reed are inside the basket. *(Figure 8)* Weave as high as you wish the basket to be, shaping the spokes as you go along. (Usually, two or three 15' weavers.)
6. To finish the basket, the top ends of the spokes must be sealed off. Take the end of any spoke, lap it over, and push it down along side of the next or the second in line. For example, number 1 may go along side number 2 or number 3. Usually, 1 into 3 and 2 into 4 is better. Continue until all are secured as in the first picture.
7. Dry. If there are any rough spots when the product is dry, sand them slightly.
8. This product may now be decorated and preserved with stain, enamel, or shellac. If the basket is to be used for a planter, an inset of a vase, glass, tin, or even foil is necessary.

Figure 2. Small reed basket

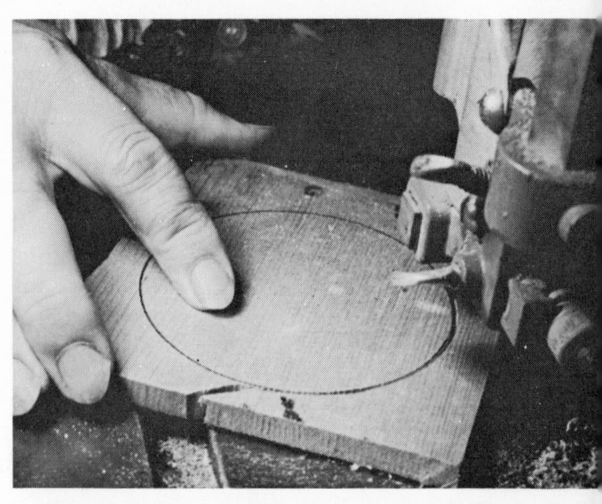

Figure 3. Round piece of quarter inch plywood or crate wood

Figure 4. Drill holes

Figure 5. Soak raffia

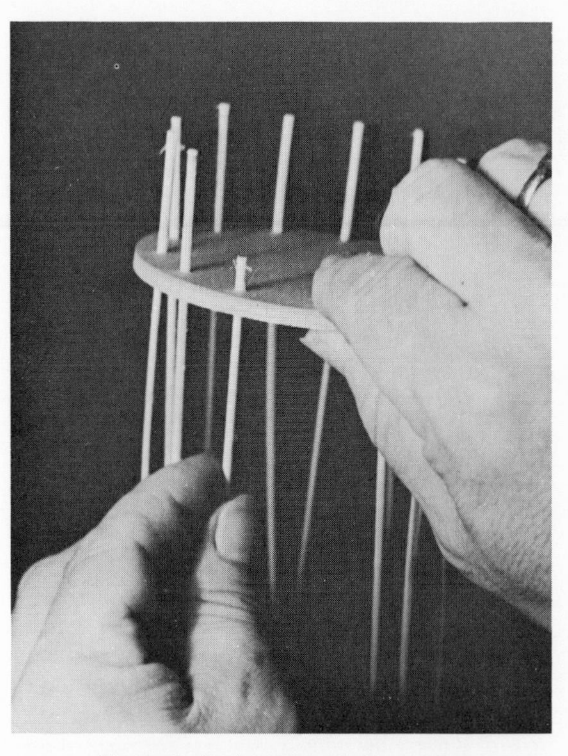

Figure 6. Push spokes through holes

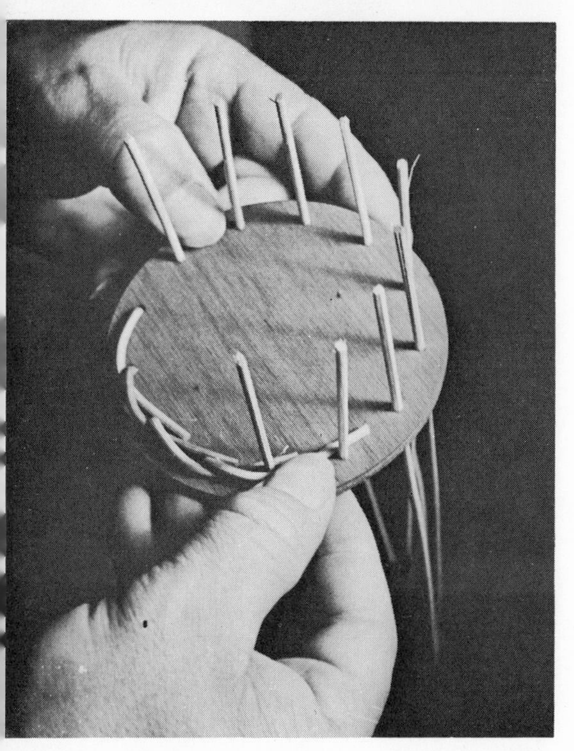

Figure 7. Weave bottom spokes around to seal off the bottom

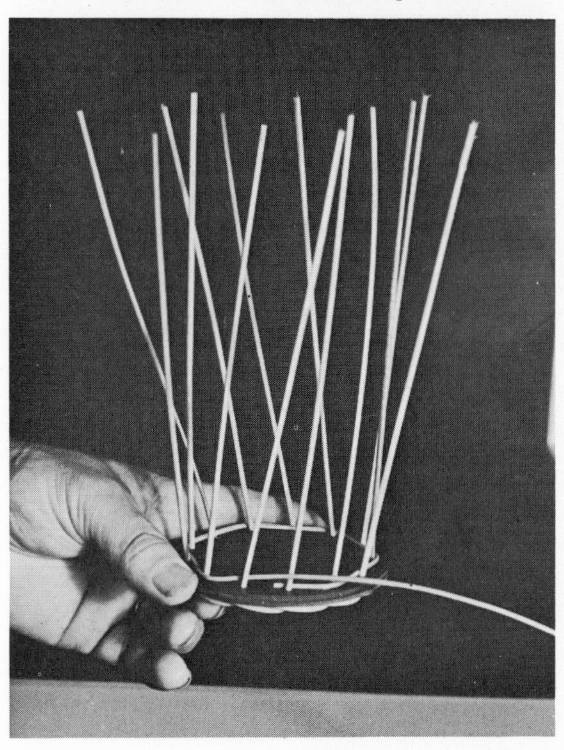

Figure 8. Weave a reed about fifteen feet long in and out among the spokes that stick up above.

PROJECT 2: REED VASE

The process is much like Project 1 except that the form does not have a wooden base. It is woven over a glass jar. *(Figure 9)*

1. Obtain a glass jar, such as a jelly jar, 3 pieces of reed about 2½' long, 1 piece 1¼' long, and 7 long pieces of weaving reed.
2. With the 3 long pieces of reed and the shorter one, form the base by placing the 3 pieces of reed like spokes of a wagon wheel and add the shorter piece to form the seventh spoke. Space these evenly so they form a wagon wheel spoke effect and render an uneven number of spokes. Secure them with string. Soak this in water along with your weavers.
3. Take a weaver and weave it in and out in a circle until you have woven a circle just slightly larger than the size of the bottom of the jelly glass. This forms the bottom.
4. Continue weaving. Set the jar on the base and weave up and around it so that the reed takes the shape of the glass. Keep the reed wet. Finish with this shape, or, if a flare at the top is desired, form it as follows: place a sauce dish or some other object which is cup-shaped on top of the jelly glass. When you weave up and around the sauce dish, the vase will be flared out at the top. This makes a vase about 8" high.
5. Finish as in Project 1 by drying the reed and shellacking.

Figure 9. Reed vase

PROJECT 3: PICTURE CARD HOLDER
(Figure 10)

1. Cut a rectangular piece of ¼" plywood for a tray 1" larger than the size of a post card (which is 3½" x 5½"). Drill 19 or 21, 1/8" holes, ¼" to ½" in from the outside edges.
2. Insert spokes approximately 6" long in the holes. Let the spokes extend about 2" on the underneath side. Soak.
3. Weave the spokes around the bottom to seal off securely. Begin with number 1 spoke. Weave the 2" lower part around the outside of number 2 spoke and lock it in front of number 3. Weave the number 2 spoke around number 3 and lock it in front of number 4. Continue until all are locked. Press the woven spokes firmly against the bottom of the base. (An example of this is *Figure 7.*)
4. Weave the top about 1" high with weavers. Put all ends inside.
5. Dry and shellac.
6. Insert a card and glass the same size as the post card if desired.

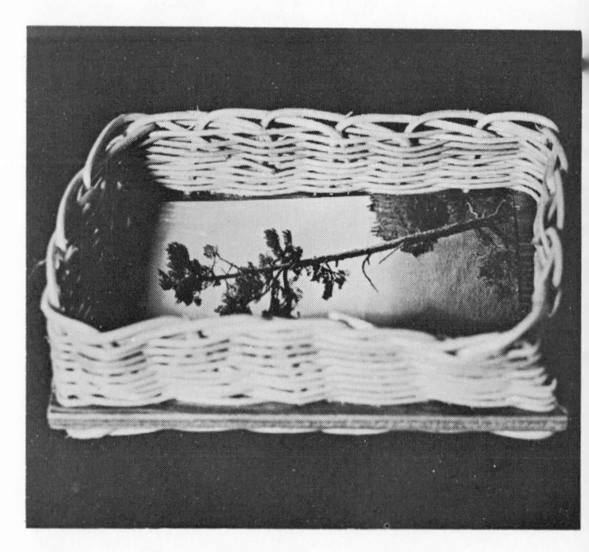

Figure 10. Picture card holder

Figure 11. Reed tray

Figure 12. Reed plate

Figure 13. Reed plate with photo added

PROJECT 4: TRAY *(Figure 11)*

1. A good size for the wood base is ¼" plywood, 13" x 19". The tray will turn out to be 12" x 18", a standard size which will accommodate standard papers. Drill 1/8" holes, ¼" to ½" in from the outside edge. Again, there must be an uneven number of holes. A good number is 59. They should be spaced approximately 1" apart.
2. Upright spokes need only be about 4–5" long, since you will not want much lap at the top for finish.
3. Follow the steps for this tray as set up in Project 3, the Picture Card Holder. (Soak spokes and weavers. Insert spokes. Finish bottom. Weave. Finish by drying and shellacking.) This forms a tray which may be plain or may hold a picture painted on standard 12" x 18" paper. Glass may also be used on top of the paper.

PROJECT 5: REED PLATE *(Figure 12)*

1. The reed plate is made by cutting a ¼" plywood base about 4¼" in diameter. Using a 1/8" drill, drill 13 evenly spaced holes into the edge of the plywood.
2. Insert reed spokes which are 10" long. Add water proof glue to the inserts to secure. These now stick out like spokes of a wagon wheel. Soak the reed.
3. Soak and bend the weavers up slightly to form a good plate shape.
4. Weave the reed weavers in and out for about 2" to 2½" (more if you want a larger plate).
5. Glue the beginning and the end weavers.
6. Finish by tucking the spokes into the second opening – 1 into 3, 2 into 4, etc.
7. Dry and shellac. Coasters may be made in the same way, only smaller. A picture may be added as in *Figure 13.*

PROJECT 6: PLANTER *(Figure 14)*

1. Use a cake or a bread pan. Cut a plywood base ½" larger all the way around. Drill holes ¼", as in the other projects. Be sure you have an uneven number of holes.
2. Insert 10" long spokes and soak.
3. Seal off the bottom by taking number 1 spoke and weaving it around number 2, then locking it in front of number 3. Weave the number 2 spoke around number 3 and lock it in front of number 4. Continue this until all are locked. Press the woven spokes firmly against the base. (See *Figure 7.*)
4. Weave the top with reed about 15' long until you have reached the height of your bread pan. Finish by inserting spokes number 1 into 3, 2 into 4, and so on.
5. Dry and shellac.

Many other projects are possible. Bread baskets, as in *Figure 15*, and vases of your choice of shape and size are easily made by following the very simple rules in the projects listed above.

Figure 14. Reed planter

Figure 15. Other shapes and sizes of your choice are entirely possible.

Materials needed:

Basics

- clay
- tub or crock for mixing and storing clay
- clean cloths and plastic to keep clay moist
- kiln
- pouring pitcher
- plaster of paris or commercial cast
- sponge (elephant ear)
- wedging board (2 boards at right angles with a wire attached from one board to the other)
- canvas
- vaseline
- rolling pin
- two 3/8" boards – about 12" long
- pencil and paper
- coffee can
- shoe box
- clothes pins
- knife
- nylon stocking or strainer

Extras

- stilts to set glazed work on in kiln
- potter's wheel and plaster head
- glaze brush (ox hair)
- spray gun and spray mask
- modeling tools (basswood)
- fettling knives
- scales

CERAMICS AND POTTERY

Ceramics is a term used to describe materials which are pliable in their natural, raw state but when dried and fired become hard and durable. Ceramics include a host of products. However, the most common use of this term is applied to *clay.*

Clay is mud, or earth. It is a material which has been used for well over 5000 years. Probably the first use of clay was for bricks by the Egyptians or, perhaps by Sargon, King of Akkad in Mesopotamia, some 2400 years before the birth of Christ.

Pottery is the term used to describe all clay vessels. China is the word used to describe the fine expensive clay ware of today. The word "china" comes from the Chinese because they were the first to produce these thin, light pieces.

Figure 1. James Wozniak at the wheel

Clay may be obtained at most craft stores. It is not unusual, however, to find people who dig it out of rich soil by river banks, for clay is earth and water. This rich soil must be purified. This is done by drying, then pulverizing, then removing all foreign matter. Next, it is mixed with water to the proper consistency for modeling. A proper consistency is plastic enough to be formed into shape and yet strong enough to hold its shape without collapsing.

Commercial clay may be purchased dry, moist, or in the form of slip (a liquid clay). If it is purchased moist or liquid, no other preparation is necessary. The dry form, however, must be mixed with the proper amount of water to make it of modeling consistency.

All clay should be prepared for modeling. First it must be *wedged*. Wedging is a process of pounding and cutting out air holes. Take a piece of clay about the size of a softball (5" or 6" in diameter). Hold the clay with both hands and cut it into two pieces against the wire of a wedging board. *(Figure 2)* Strike the pieces together again; cut again. Repeat this process until no air holes show in the two halves. *(Figure 3)* Also knead and pound the clay. *(Figure 4)* The clay should then be ready to model, press, or throw on the potter's wheel.

The following are six projects which can be formed with prepared clay, or slip, and fired to completion. The firing process will be explained at the end of this chapter.

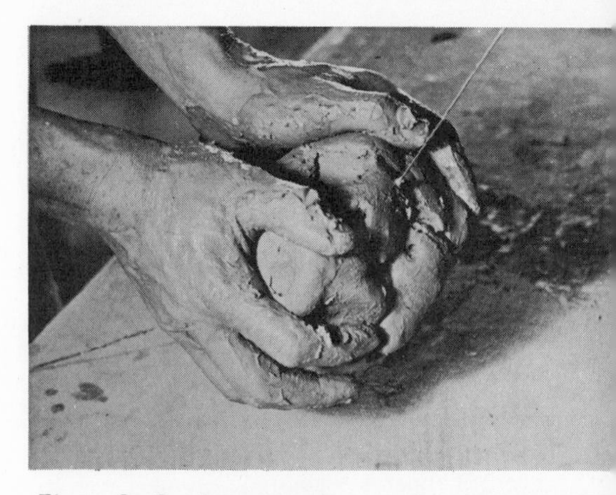

Figure 2. Cut into two pieces against the wire of a wedging board.

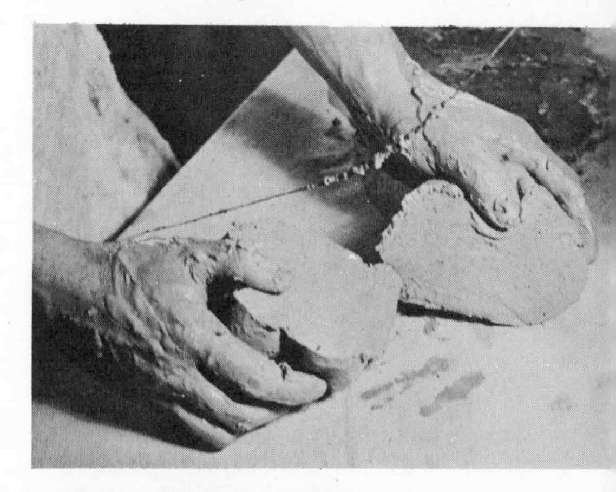

Figure 3. Repeat cutting process until no holes show in the two halves.

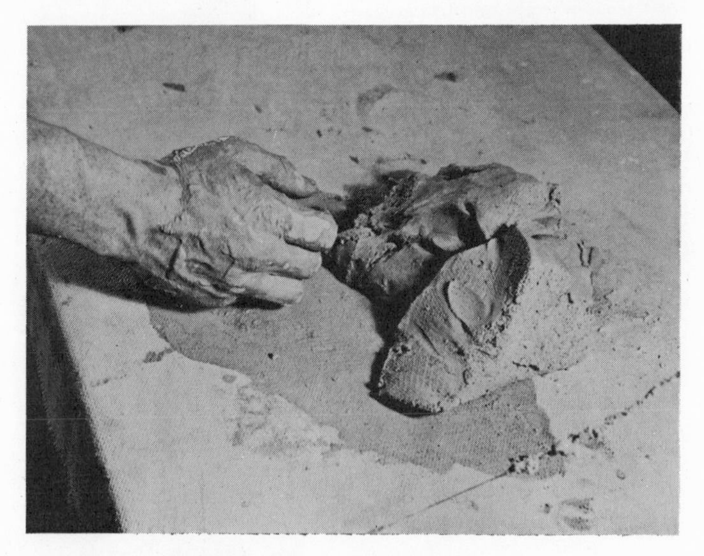

Figure 4. Knead and pound the clay.

PROJECT 1: PINCH POT VASE *(Figure 5)*

The pinch method is the most simple way to form clay into a shape. It is used by children and beginners and is a good way to get the "feel" of clay. It is easy and takes little time.

1. Select a lump of clay about the size of your fist.
2. Form this into a ball, making it as smooth as possible. *(Figure 6)*
3. Hold the ball in the palm of the hand and work your thumb in the center around and around. Press deeper into the clay with each turn. *(Figure 7)*
4. Form and smooth the edges. *(Figure 8)* Try to keep the thickness of all parts even. Slowly rotate the clay to work on all parts at once. Watch for cracks and checks. When finished, the dish should be about ¼" thick and even.
5. When it is smooth, scratch your name or initials and the date on the bottom.
6. Dry. Do not dry rapidly or with artificial heat or blower.
7. When the piece becomes leather hard, you may be able to improve its shape and smoothness.
8. Dry completely.
9. Fire. (See the end of the chapter.)

Figure 5. Pinch pot vase

Figure 6. Forming pinch pot from ball

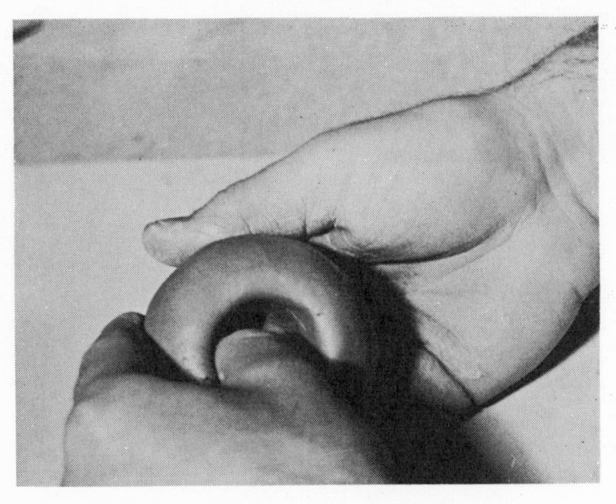

Figure 7. Turning pinch pot and pressing thumb in

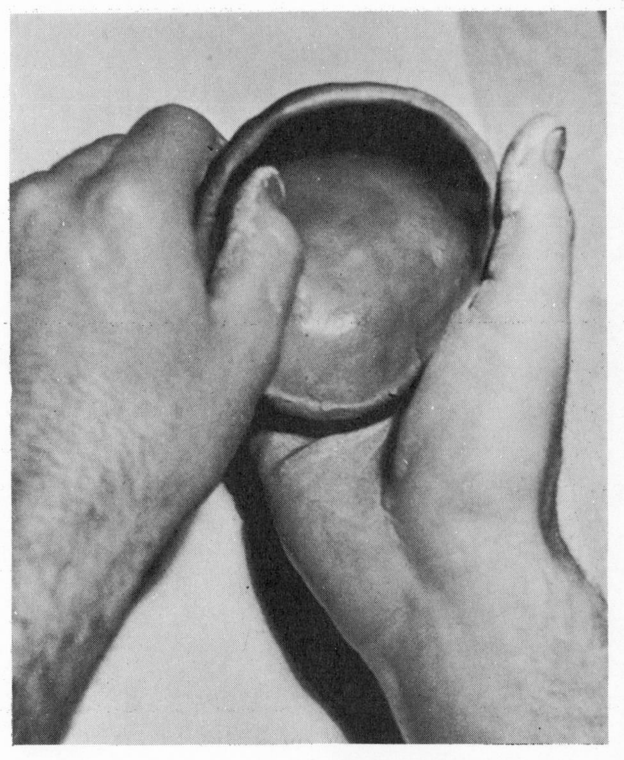

Figure 8. Form smooth edges of the pinch pot

PROJECT 2: COIL POT *(Figure 9)*

Figure 9. Coil pot

The coil method is a little more difficult than the pinch pot. It is the method used by natives of Southwest United States, Mexico, and other countries where machinery has not been introduced extensively.

1. Select a lump of clay and form it into a ball.
2. Press this ball down to form a bottom or base. The thickness should be about 1" or less.
3. Take another lump of clay and roll it into a coil.
4. Place this coil onto the base and form it around and around the base. *(Figures 10 and 11)* It is wise to score and cement the coil to the base with slip clay. The consistency of slip clay should be similar to thick cream. Strive for symmetry. Use several coils to form the pot to the desired height. A template or pattern may be used to insure symmetry.
5. Blend each coil together to form a smooth surface.
6. Rub slip clay over the inside and outside.
7. Smooth with a sponge.
8. Dry.
9. Fire. (See the end of the chapter.)

Figure 10. Place coil on base and form it around and around.

Figure 11. Continue with coil

PROJECT 3: DRAPED DISH *(Figure 12)*

The draped method is also called the sling method. It consists of rolling prepared clay with a rolling pin and draping it over a form.

1. Choose a ball of clay, diameter about 5" or 6".
2. Place it on a canvas covered table between two sticks of equal size, about 1/8" to 1/4" thick. The thickness of sticks insures an even piece.
3. Roll out the clay ball on the canvas to form a flat sheet of clay. *(Figure 13)*
4. Set the piece to be draped on the sticks and lift the clay slab. *(Figure 14)*
5. Lay the slab over a dish form and trim the edges. *(Figure 15)*
6. Rub the slip over the form to smooth.
7. Do any additional smoothing with a sponge.
8. Dry. Remove from the form before entirely dry because there is a possibility that it will crack as it shrinks.
9. Fire. (See the end of the chapter.)

Figure 12. Draped dish

Figure 13. Roll out ball to form clay into a flat sheet.

Figure 14. Set pieces to be draped on sticks and lift up the clay slab.

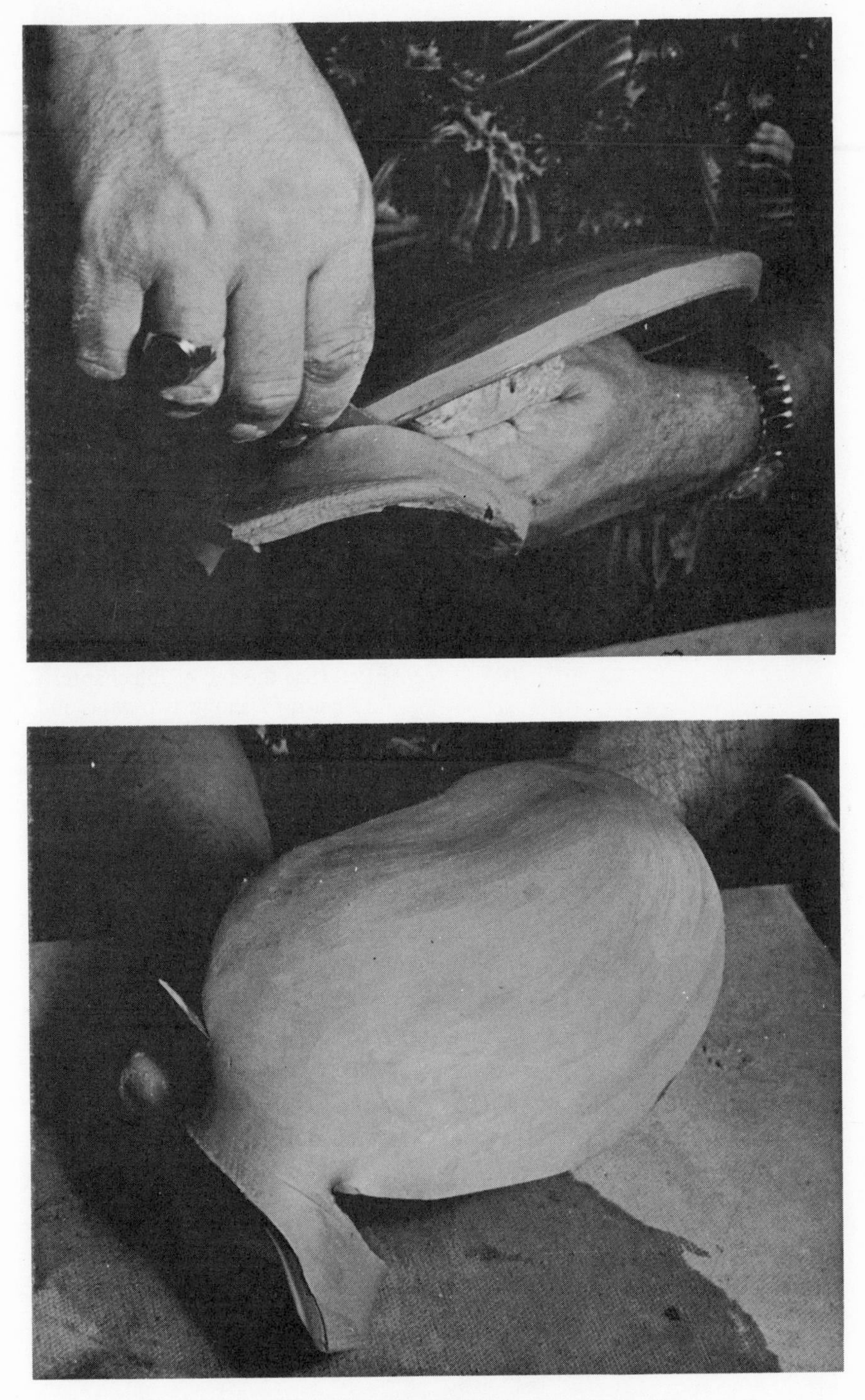

Figure 15. Lay slab over dish form and trim the edges.

PROJECT 4: SLAB ASH TRAY *(Figure 16)*

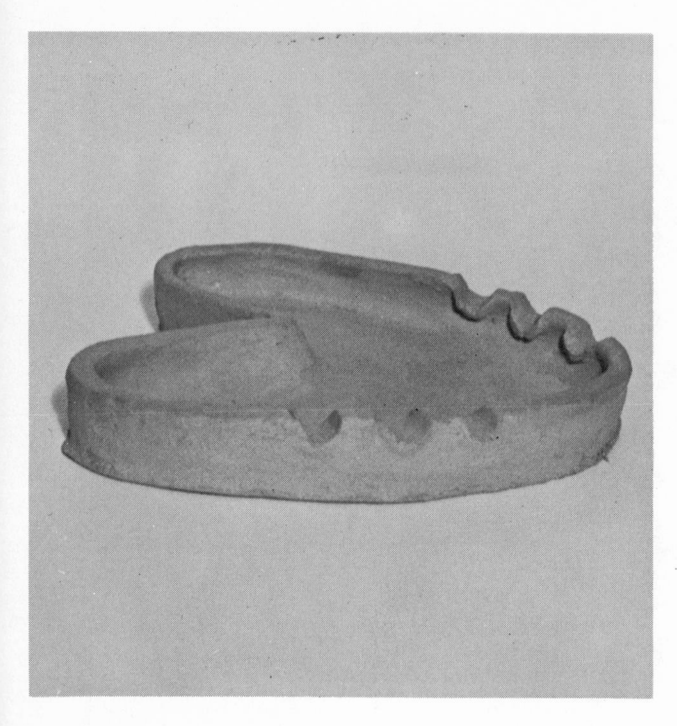

The slab method is like the sling or drape method. The piece is formed by working together rolled out slabs of clay.

1. Choose clay balls about 5" in diameter.
2. Place the balls between sticks about 1/8" or 1/4" thick.
3. Roll the balls into slabs.
4. Place a predrawn paper pattern on the slab, and cut out this shape.
5. Cut out long, narrow, flat slabs to be used on the sides. Be sure they are long enough to reach completely around the base. They should be as wide as the article is deep.
6. Score the top edge of the bottom and apply a thick layer of slip.
7. Attach the sides. Weld the outside edge of the bottom to the sides with a modeling tool or knife. The ends of the sides are joined together in the same way. To make the inside joints secure, roll out a long, thin coil of clay and work this into the inside corners where sides meet the base. Smooth.
8. Dry.
9. Fire. (See the end of the chapter.)

Figure 17 shows two vases and tiles done in the above method.

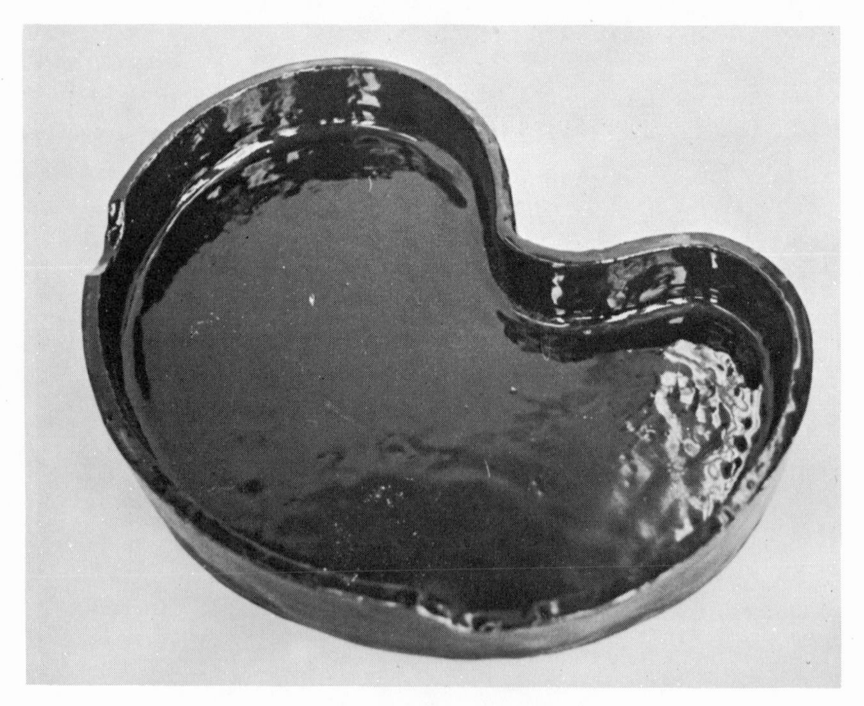

Figure 16. Slab ash tray

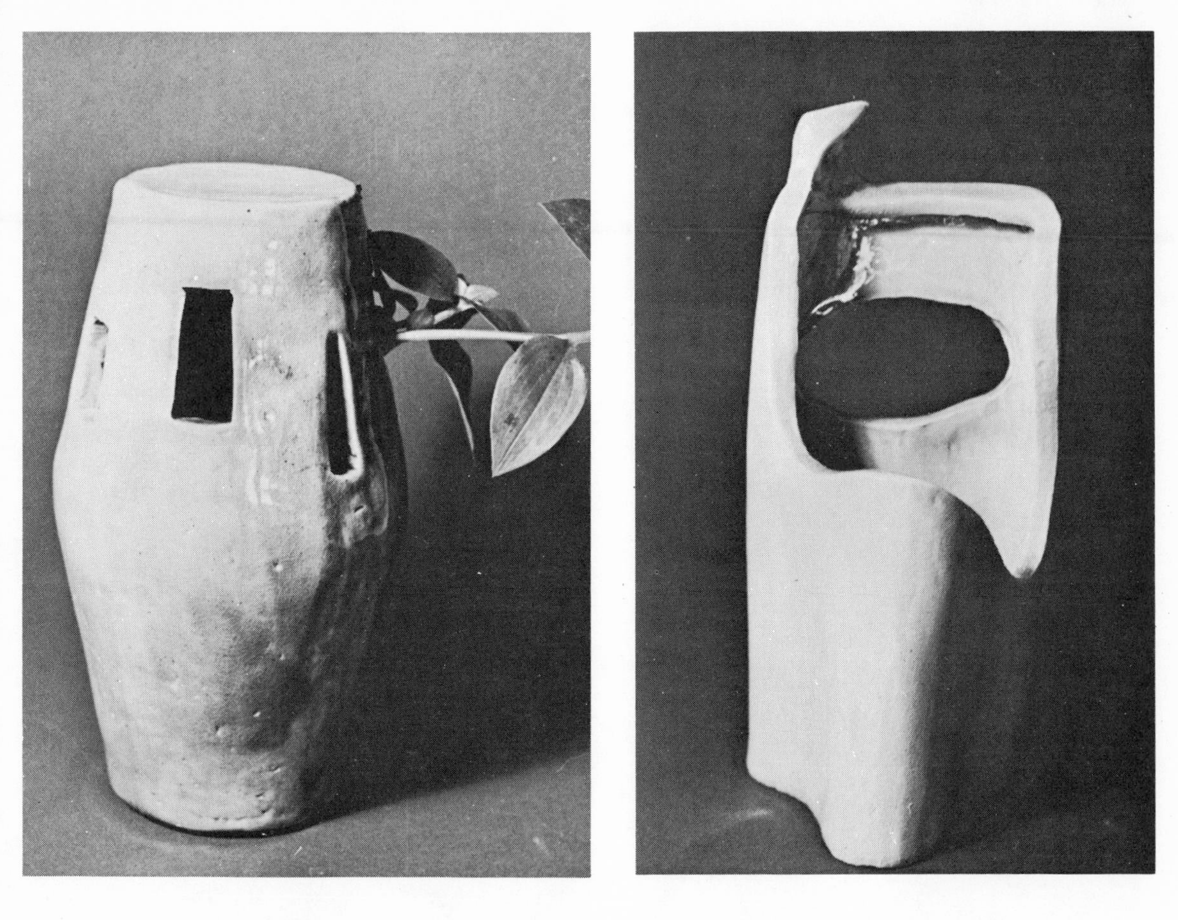

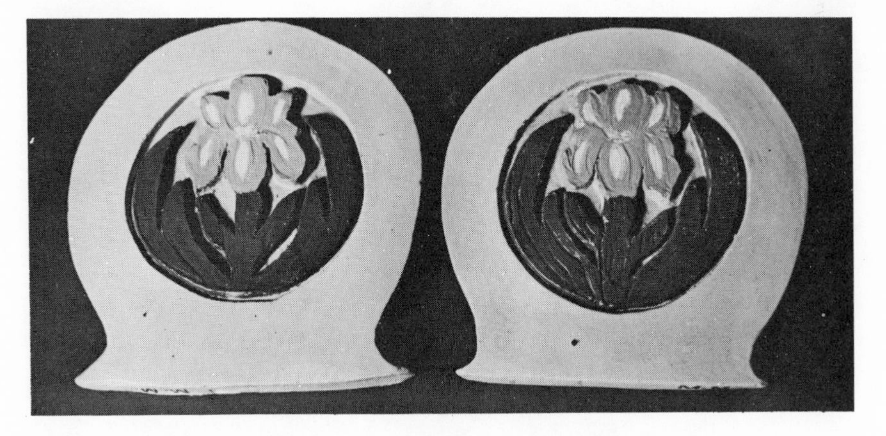

Figure 17. Two vases and tiles – slab formed objects

PROJECT 5: SLIP CAST VASE *(Figure 18)*

Much of the commercial ware today is made by the slip casting process. Slip is a mixture of clay and water of about the consistency of heavy cream. It is poured into a plaster of paris mold. The plaster absorbs the water and leaves a shell of clay to form the shape. This method is very popular with beginners because it is easy and produces a professional looking result. Slip can be prepared from clay, but it is wiser to buy ready-mixed slip.

1. Prepare or buy slip.
2. Prepare a plaster mold. Be sure the mold is thoroughly dry and clean.
3. Grease the mold well with vaseline or another lubricant. *(Figure 19)* Do not grease the part to be cast.
4. Fasten the mold together securely. *(Figure 20)* Place it on several thicknesses of newspapers.
5. Stir the slip thoroughly and strain. *(Figure 21)* Use a nylon stocking or a 40 or 50 mesh sieve. Be sure there is enough slip to fill the mold completely.
6. Pour the slip slowly and steadily until the mold is full. Do not let it run over. *(Figure 22)*
7. Leave the slip in the mold until the proper thickness is obtained. Tip the mold gently and observe the thickness of the hardened clay around the top. The time may vary from a few minutes for small pieces to twenty minutes or more depending on several factors: (a) the dryness of the mold, (b) the thickness of the slip, and (c) the desired thickness for the finished piece.
8. When the desired thickness is reached, pour out the excess slip. Leave the mold upside down to let the slip drain evenly.
9. Leave the mold until the clay becomes hard enough to remove without damage. Large molds may take several hours. *(Figure 23)*
10. Let the piece harden somewhat, then clean it from mold marks. *(Figure 24)* Handle it carefully because it is very fragile at this stage. *(Figure 25)* *Figure 26* shows the fish form also done by this process.
11. Dry.
12. Fire. (See the end of the chapter.)

Figure 18. Slip cast vase

Figure 19. Grease mold. Do not grease part to be cast.

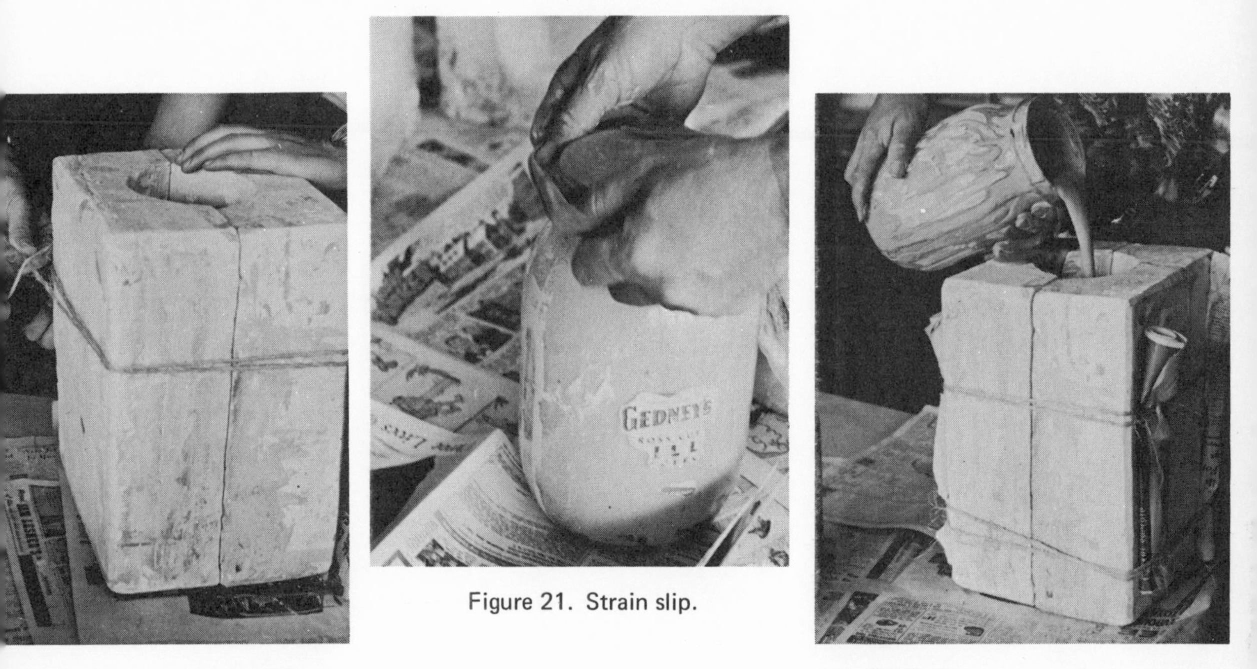

Figure 21. Strain slip.

ure 20. Fasten mold together.

Figure 22. Pour slip into mold.

Figure 23. Leave clay in mold several hours after opening.

Figure 24. Let pieces harden somewhat before cleaning.

Figure 25. Handle carefully

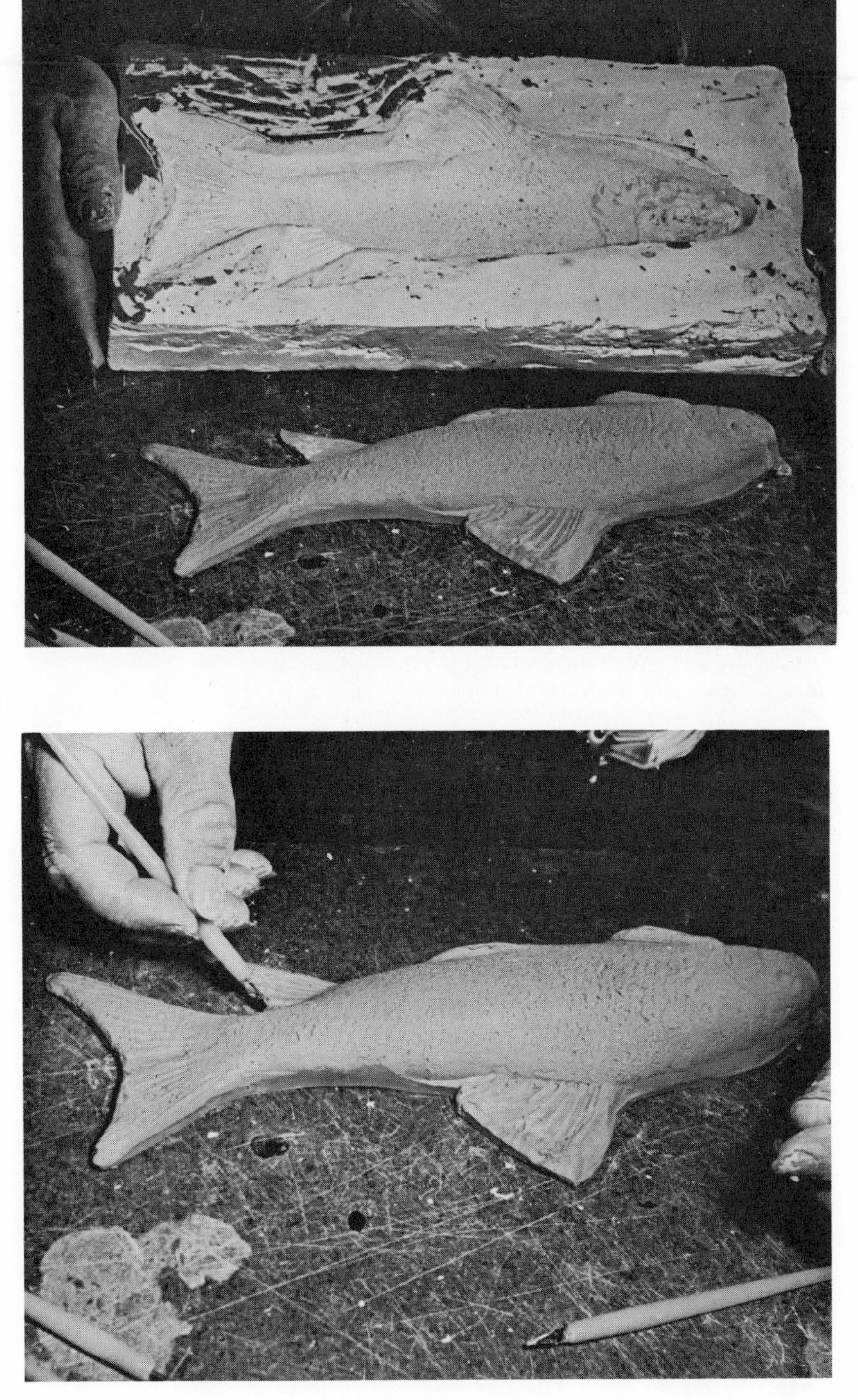

Figure 26. Fish mold

PROJECT 6: THROWING ON THE POTTER'S WHEEL *(Figure 27* executed by James Wozniak*)*

For years the "throwing" method has been the height and symbol of the ceramic art. This process is the ultimate goal of nearly every person interested in pottery. There is no substitute for the wheel method where uniqueness, beauty, and originality are sought. This process usually requires years of experience for one to become expert. There are electric powered wheels on the market but many of the true ceramic craftsmen still prefer the old "kick" type wheel since the process of "throwing" involves the whole body. The "kick" wheel presents a challenge of total muscular coordination and mental concentration in addition to that of the skill of the hand.

1. Prepare the clay as explained. (Page 22)
2. Set a commercial plaster head on the very center of the wheel. *(Figure 28)* Fasten this head onto the wheel securely with clay.
3. Form the lump of clay into a ball and throw it down on the wheel head as near the center as possible.
4. Center the clay by forcing the ball of clay into the exact center of the wheel (while rotating the wheel) by using the heel of one hand and fingers of the other. *(Figure 29)* Downward pressure should be applied to keep the clay from loosening and coming off the head. Keep your hands very wet all through the process.
5. When the clay is centered, force it up into a cone or cylindrical shape, then push it back down. *(Figure 30)* Do this several times.
6. Now the clay is ready to open. Place both hands around the clay and gently force both thumbs down into the center. Leave at least ½" at the bottom. *(Figure 31)* Remember to keep the hands wet and the motions steady but gentle.
7. When the piece is opened, it is ready to draw up. Place the index finger of the left hand on the inside and the right on the outside. *(Figure 32)* This pressure will force the ball into shape. Slowly and carefully pull the hands upward. Do not use too much pressure or you will break the walls or throw it off center. Hold your hands rigid. Form the piece several inches high and keep the thickness even.
8. Next, form the piece as shown in *Figure 33.* (If a lip or spout is to be formed, gently pull a finger over one edge of the piece while holding both sides with the other hand.)

Figure 27. Wheel formed pot (by James Wozniak)

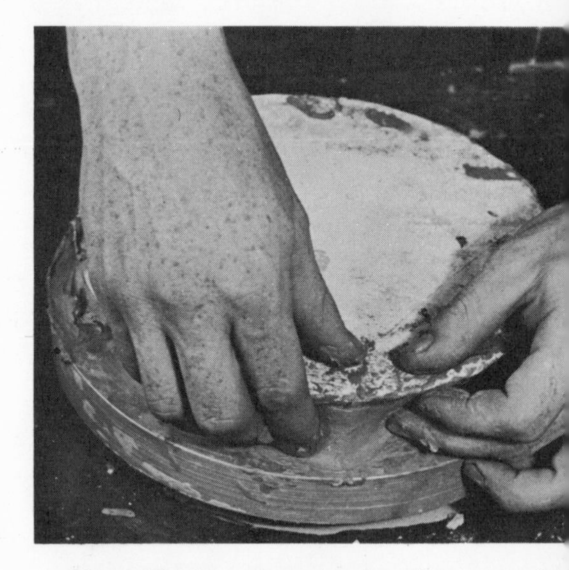

Figure 28. Set a plaster head on the center of th

Figure 29. Center the clay.

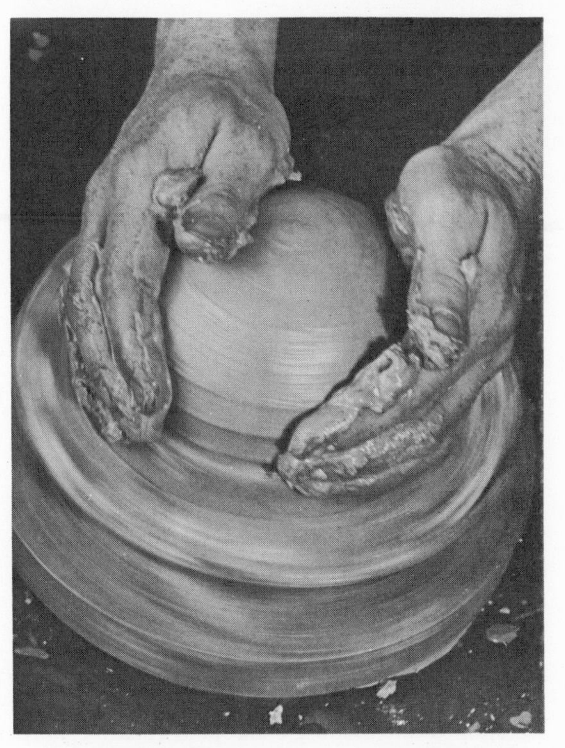

Figure 30. Force the clay up into a cone.

Figure 31. Open the clay.

9. Dry. Remove the piece from the plaster head by sliding a wire under it.
10. Finish. When the piece is leather hard, place it upside down on the wheel (centered). Fasten with several pieces of oil base clay. With the use of a knife or tool, smooth and trim the base as desired (usually a spiral cut is inserted to form a ridge for the foot of the piece.) Smooth it all over with a damp sponge.
11. Fire.

Firing is done (usually in commercial kilns) when the formed piece is bone dry. The first firing is called *bisque*. This firing changes the clay into a ceramic product, and it becomes hard and durable.

1. Be sure all ware is thoroughly dry. Drying may take from one day to several weeks, depending on the size of the piece and the atmospheric conditions.
2. Stack the kiln. *(Figure 34)* In bisque firing the greenware pieces may touch and do not need to be placed on stilts. Close the kiln and do not open until the firing is complete and objects are cool.
3. Turn the kiln on low for an hour or two, then bring the heat up gradually. Leave the peep hole open for the first period of firing to allow moisture to escape. No piece should be thicker than 1". Most clay matures at about 1900° F. Commercial clays will indicate the firing temperature.
4. Turn off the kiln when bisque has reached the maturing temperature. Most kilns with pyrometers have automatic gauges for shut off.
5. Cool until the temperature registers 0°. Open the kiln a little at a time.
6. Remove pieces from the kiln and put them in a clean dry place.
7. Apply the glaze (paint, spray, dip, or pour). *(Figure 35)*
8. Glaze fire. When stacking the kiln with glazed pieces place them on stilts and be sure no piece touches another or the edge of the kiln. Glaze firing temperature may be brought up rapidly. Each glaze will indicate its firing temperature.
9. Turn the kiln off (or watch to be sure that the automatic pyrometer shuts off the kiln.)
10. Cool.
11. Remove the finished pieces.

New and amazingly unique methods of finish for clay are now being practiced. For example, after bisque firing, paint a tempera color on the once fired piece. When this is dry, cover it with shoe polish, using a rag, and polish. *(Figure 36)*

Clay is a wonderful craft for hobbyists, craftsmen, school groups, and children, as well as adult education programs, home crafts, camps, and clubs. It offers a simple medium of satisfaction easily achieved by most anyone and is an extremely creative avenue of pursuit for the most gifted.

Figure 32. Draw the clay up.

Figure 33. Keep thicknesses even and form the piece.

Finished thrown pots by Harlan Owens and Richard Joslin.

Figure 34. Stack the kiln

Figure 35. Apply glaze

Figure 36. Tempera color polished with shoe polish

Figure 37. Finished vases and pitcher; oil base model

Materials needed:

Basics

- kiln
- 18 gauge copper
- oil (trinket)
- glass-powder, chunks, threads
- clean paper
- fine sand paper or emery paper
- cleanser or steel wool
- asbestos board
- tweezers
- solder (rosin core)
- file
- old nylon stocking to use as a sifter
- cloth (rags)
- spatula
- plastic spray or colorless nail polish
- findings (earring backs, cuff link backs, pin backs, etc.)
- copper chain for medallions

Extras

- scissors
- copper jewelry wire
- metal shears or jewelry saw
- crackle liquid glaze
- long-handled metal fork or spear
- asbestos gloves

COPPER ENAMELING

An exciting craft which has attracted wide attention the last few years is that of enameling on copper. This craft was practiced many years before the birth of Christ and has continued with varying degrees of popularity through the centuries. Children, as well as adults, are able to create in this medium. Children as young as nine and ten years of age are able to produce jewelry of merit. Older people find it an intriguing hobby, as well as an opportunity for creative expression. New designs and techniques continually present themselves. By the addition of variations to basic designs, beautiful and unique articles can be made.

The basic enameling process is simple. It consists of fusing or firing glass onto copper at a temperature of about 1300°F. The base for enameling is *copper*–pure, 18 gauge. (Thinner copper is more likely to warp, and heavier copper is more difficult to form.) Pre-formed shapes for ash trays, cuff links, and earrings are obtainable at most craft stores, or the creator may cut his own shapes from sheet copper with tin shears. The glass which is applied to copper can be obtained in chunk, powder, or thread form. Kilns for heating range from 3", to 8" x 10" or larger.

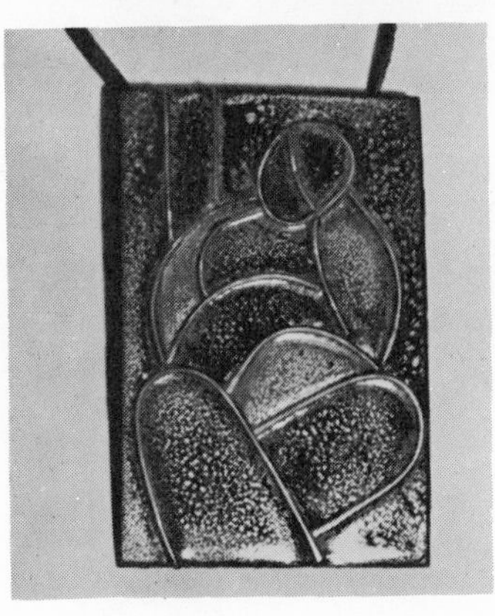

Figure 1. Medallions and earrings

PROJECT 1: SIMPLE EARRINGS *(Figure 2)*

Choose pre-formed copper shapes – two alike, round, square, or oval of the size you like. You will find that they come in sizes of ½", ¾", 1", and larger.

1. Clean the metal, using a cleanser, vinegar and salt, or steel wool. *(Figure 3)* Wash, wipe dry, and do not touch the clean surface.
2. Apply oil to the clean surface. *(Figure 4)* This oil accompanies enamel kits or can be purchased at craft stores.
3. Apply the powder. Dust powdered glass of the desired color over the entire top surface. *(Figure 5)* Dust the powder through a sifter or a fine nylon stocking. Apply uniformly and thick enough so that copper does not show through. Enamel may also be applied with a spatula, the stencil method, or by pouring, dipping, spraying, or painting. The dusting method is the easiest. If the excess powder is clean, it may be returned to the bottle.
4. Fire the piece by placing it carefully with a spatula in a pre-heated kiln. *(Figure 6)* Fire in the kiln for approximately three minutes. Watch the coating. It will appear powdery, turn sugary, then become smooth and shiny when matured. Remove it from the heat by slipping a spatula under it.
5. Cool on a piece of asbestos. *(Figure 7)* You will notice that during the cooling process the colors will change. When the copper is cool, the top surface will be completely covered with a smooth, shiny, hard surface of colored glaze which is the powdered glass fused to the copper. No design has been executed here, and this is the simplest method. However, you may find the simple solid color a pleasant and desirable result. Enamels of obtainable glazes vary in color and are available in transparent and opaque types.
6. Finish. Carefully clean the back and edges with sand paper, and file (as shown in *Figure 8*) until all the fire scale is removed and the piece is clean and a pinkish copper color on the back and edges. Be gentle. Remember you are working with glass. Be sure when filing that you file away from the glass, not toward it, for filing can chip the glass off the copper.
7. Solder. (For pin backs, earrings, cuff link findings, etc.) The simplest soldering processes are effected right on top of the smallest, cheapest kiln (called "trinket"), as illustrated in *Figure 9.* This little kiln has a tin top and is obtainable at most craft departments. Use rosin core solder. Attach the finding by laying the clean copper piece upside down on the trinket kiln top. This will not hurt the glaze. Apply a very small piece of rosin core solder (about 1/16"). Heat. Place the clean finding on the melted solder. Remove from the heat, using tweezers. Press the finding on to the copper back until cool and the solder is set. Remember all surfaces must be clean in order to be soldered. Other soldering methods are possible, but this one is the easiest.
8. Final finish. Polish the cool copper backs with steel wool. Spray with a fine tarnish resistant or paint with clear nail enamel. The earrings are now finished. They are clear, plain jewelry with no decoration.

Figure 2. Finished plain coppers

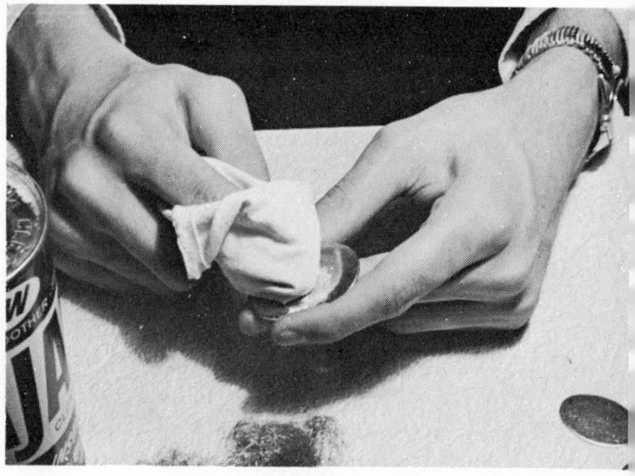

Figure 3. Cleaning

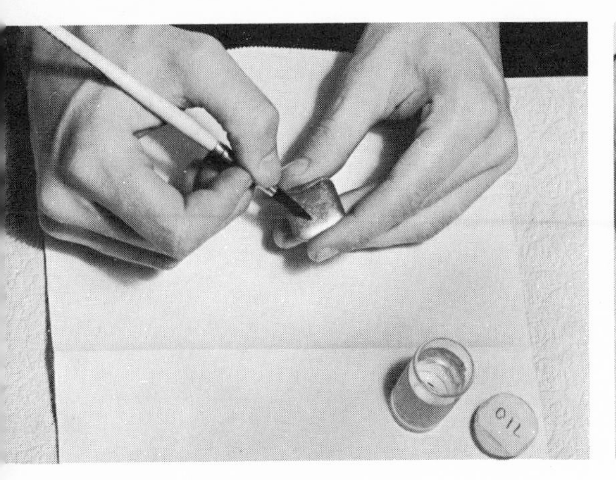

Figure 4. Oil

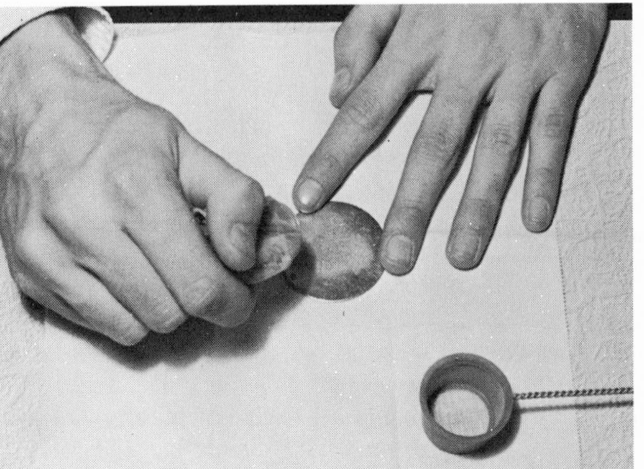

Figure 5. Dust powder

Figure 6. Fire

Figure 7. Cool on asbestos

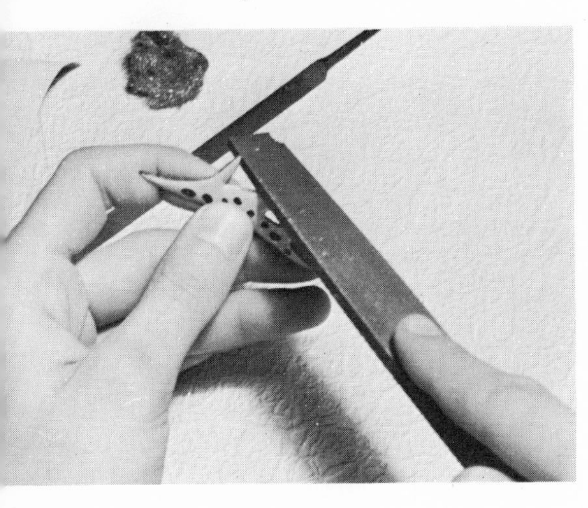

Figure 8. File

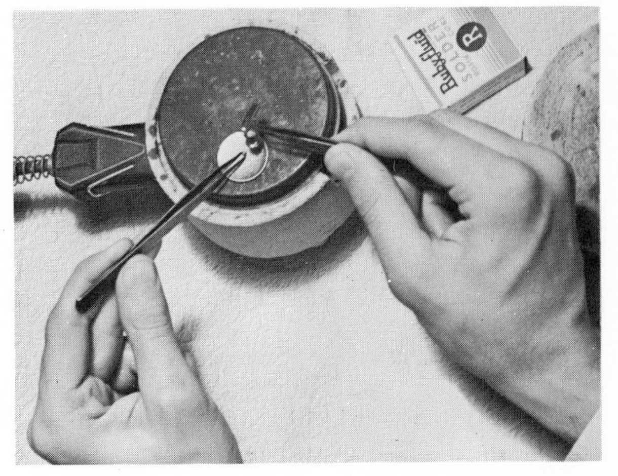

Figure 9. Solder

PROJECT 2: CUFF LINKS WITH SIMPLE, DISTURBED DESIGN

Again, as in Project 1, use pre-formed shapes in the size desired for cuff links. Follow the procedures of steps 1, 2, and 3, as in Project 1. Next, continue with the following:

1. For the design, use tweezers and place several small colored glass threads or chunks in the center of the powdered copper. *(Figure 10)*
2. Fire. Follow as in Project 1, however, when the article becomes smooth and shiny, disturb the chunks with a long-handled metal fork or spear. Asbestos gloves will be handy because the kiln becomes very hot. Do not leave open spaces of exposed copper or the copper will burn and appear rough and dull, spoiling the shine of smooth baked enamel. If this disturbing process causes the surface to be rough and bumpy, fire a minute longer and the bumps will melt down. This process demands no design or talent but produces a lovely, abstract, and interesting design. *(Figure 11)*
3. Finish as described in Project 1. If you wish to do this in two firings, proceed as in Project 1 to get the base glaze coat. When this is cool, paint a little oil on the fired enamel and place the glass chunks. (The oil will keep the chunks from sliding off.) Now proceed as given above in Project 2, Step 2.

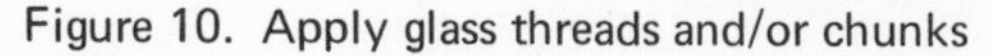

Figure 10. Apply glass threads and/or chunks

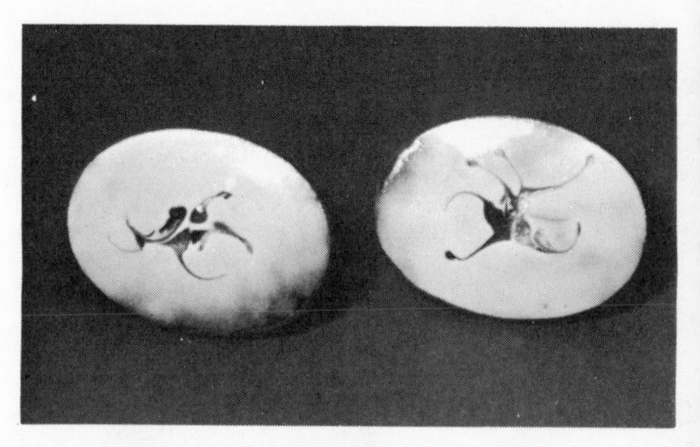

Figure 11. Disturbed-design cuff links

PROJECT 3: ASH TRAY WITH GLASS THREADS AND/OR STONES

The little trinket kiln will take 3" ash trays, but a bigger kiln is needed for ash trays 4" and larger. Follow the first three steps of Project 1.

1. With your tweezers apply glass threads and/or small chunks in an interesting design. *(Figure 12)*
2. Finish as in Project 1, Steps 6–9.

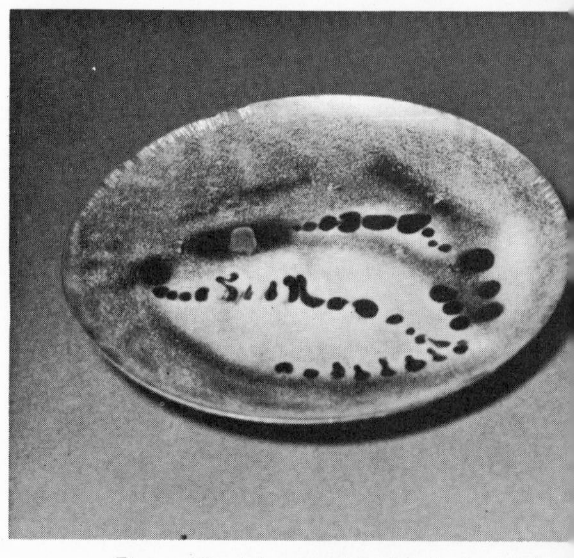

Figure 12. Ash tray with chunks (stones)

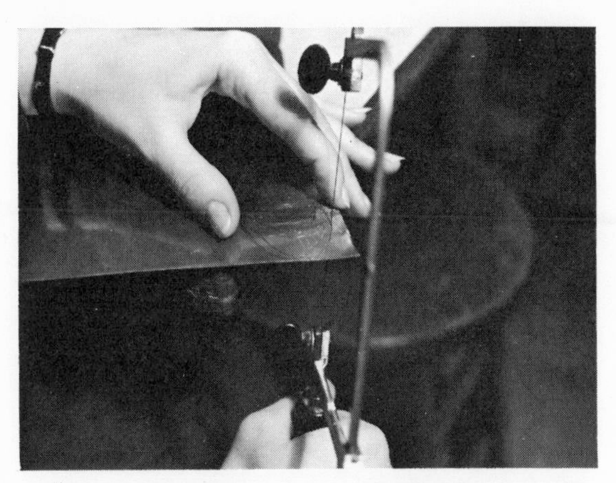

Figure 13. Cut copper

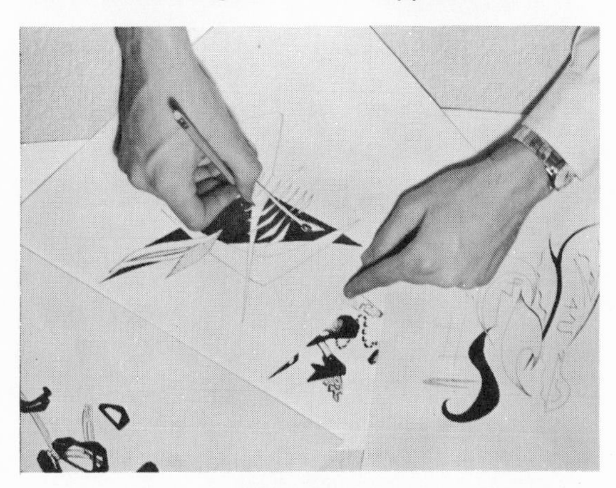

Figure 14. Drawing black and white designs for copper shapes

Figure 15. Medallion (copper wire). Chain is also hand-made of single loops

PROJECT 4: MEDALLION WITH COPPER WIRE

Pre-formed pieces suitable for a medallion are usually circular and at least 2" in diameter with a hole drilled at the top. The medallion project is also suited for advanced pupils who like to cut their own shapes. Cut copper with metal shears or a jeweler's saw. *(Figure 13)* Some interesting shapes for medallions are shown in *Figure 14*. Designs for the medallion may be like those suggested in Project 1, 2, and 3, but the application of copper wire is very effective. Preparation is again the same as the basic steps listed in the other projects. Complete as follows:

1. When the powder is applied evenly, carefully place a design of copper wire (which has been previously formed) on the powdered surface. Use your tweezers.
2. Fire. It is sometimes advisable to press the wire down into its enamel bed. Do this when the glaze bed is shiny, and it will better assure its attachment.
3. Cool.
4. Finish as described in the other projects. When cleaning this jewelry, file the top of the copper wire to clean off the fire scale. *(Figure 15)*
5. This naturally requires no soldering unless you wish the medallion to have a pin back as well as a chain. The medallion, however, must have a chain affixed. Loop a jump ring through the hole in the medallion. (Jump rings are small; ½", ¼", and 1/16" copper rings are available at craft stores or made at home with copper jeweler's wire.) Also loop it through the copper chain which you have chosen. Close the ring. Because of this jump ring, the medallion will lie flat. Use jump rings to fasten the chain together. Most medallions hang low, so the chain should be long enough to be slipped over the head with no spring ring necessary for opening and closing the back fastener. The chain should be about 24" long to go over the head. If it is shorter, a spring ring fastener will be needed. Spring rings can be obtained at craft stores. Also available are other copper findings which can be affixed simply by looping them into the jump rings.
6. Finish as described in Project 1, Steps 6–8.

PROJECT 5: STENCIL DESIGN

Figure 16. Stencil

Prepare a pre-formed pin or cut one out of copper as described in other projects, Steps 1–3.

1. Cut a design out of fairly stiff paper and place it on a once fired object. (Use oil for security in holding the paper stencil.) Dust another color over the stencil-covered surface. Carefully remove the stencil, using tweezers. Fire again. (The dusting of the second color can be done before the first firing if you wish. See *Figure 16.*)
2. Finish as described in Project 1, Steps 6–8.

PROJECT 6: CRACKLE PROCESS (for any cup-shaped piece)

1. Use a cup-shaped piece of copper. Prepare as usual and fire as explained in Project 1, for a plain color surface.
2. Cool.
3. Apply a coat of liquid crackle glaze of the appropriate color. Let this dry thoroughly.
4. Fire, as in the directions for crackle glaze, for one minute.
5. Remove from the fire. As the piece cools, it will crackle into an interesting design. The design may be applied on either the concave or the convex side. *(Figure 17)*

The preceding were six simple suggestions for variations in copper enameling. They are easy processes, and, as you experiment with them, you will be thrilled with your results and eager to investigate further. One success leads to another. Some of the books of merit on enameling are listed in the bibliography.

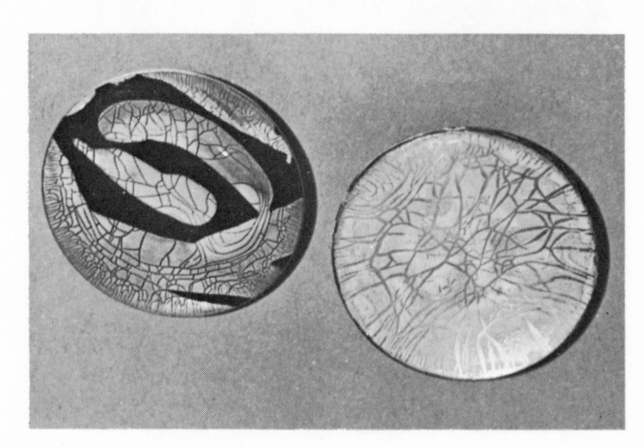

Figure 17. Crackle glaze ash trays

LEATHER

Leathercraft is known to be over three thousand years old, yet it is still exciting and fascinating. One's leisure time can be enjoyable and worthwhile through the creation of useful and good looking leather products.

Leather, or pelts of animals, are classified according to their sizes. A hide comes from an animal such as a horse or cow. Kips come from the same animals, but are undersized. Skins come from small animals such as goats, sheep, and calves. Pelts are tanned to make them tough and flexible and to prevent decomposition. Most leather is either vegetable or chrome tanned. If tooling or carving is to be done, the leather must be vegetable tanned because chrome tanned leather is not toolable. Leather may be finished in its own natural, distinctive grain, or the grain may be imitated by being embossed or sueded.

Leather may be purchased :

a. by the whole or half hide at a specific price per square foot. This is desirable when using a large quantity because it is usually cheaper.
b. by the square foot. This method of buying small quantities of leather is somewhat more expensive.
c. by kits. Companies furnish kits containing all the materials and instructions for a project. The kit limits experience in design, layout, and cut out.
d. by the pound. Some companies have small pieces which they sell by the pound. It is very inexpensive and a good source for making small items.

The basic processes are relatively simple. They consist of layout and cutout, tooling and modeling, assembly, and finishing. Designs may be made upon the leather by tooling and carving impressions, burning or branding the surface, or dyeing. The design should afford an opportunity for creative expression. New designs and techniques can be developed if a little imagination and experimentation are used.

The materials needed are leather, keyplate, snap fasteners, lacing, and rubber cement. Sometimes a sponge is handy. The following projects are arranged in a progression from simple to more complex. It is a good idea to store leather in a clean plastic bag. Follow the steps listed below and you will have no trouble completing the projects with satisfying results.

Figure 1. Leather briefcase

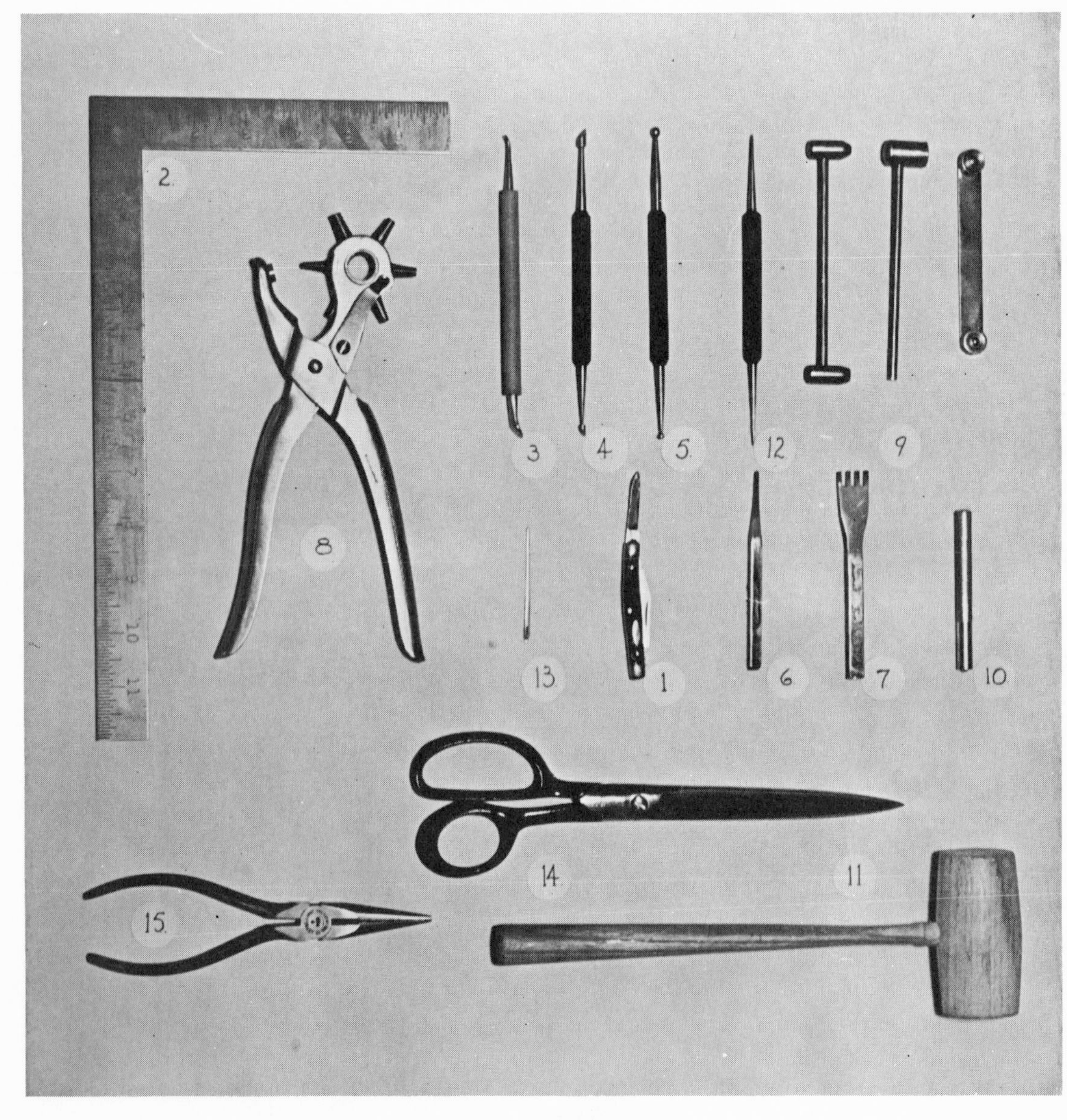

Figure 2. Materials

Tools needed for Leather Craft: *(Figure 2)*

Tool	Alternate Item	Use
1. skiving knife	single-edged razor blade	cutting and thinning leather
2. right angle rule	framing square	measuring and squaring the leather
3. modeler or tracer	wooden skewer	tracing, tooling and stippling design
4. deerfoot modeler		beveling and setting down backgrounds
5. ball end modeler		embossing and texturing
6. one-pronged thonging chisel	an 8-penny nail filed to a flat point	making slits for lacing
7. four-pronged thonging chisel		equally spacing slits for lacing
8. revolving punch	drive punch	used for punching round holes
9. snap fasteners		to set snaps
10. eyelet setter		to set eyelets
11. mallet		striking stamps, setting eyelets and fastening snaps
12. stippler	a sharp pointed instrument	texturing backgrounds
13. lacing needle		to guide lace through slits
14. shears	kitchen shears	cutting light weight leather
15. lacing pliers	household pliers	pulling laces in hard to reach places

(Tools should be kept clean because they will mark the raw leather and create a cleaning problem.)

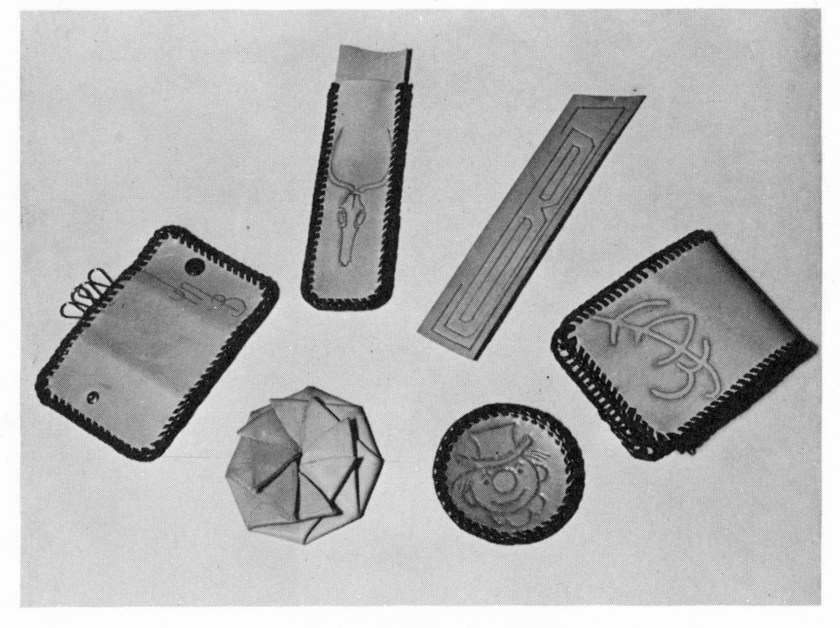

Figure 3. Suggested projects

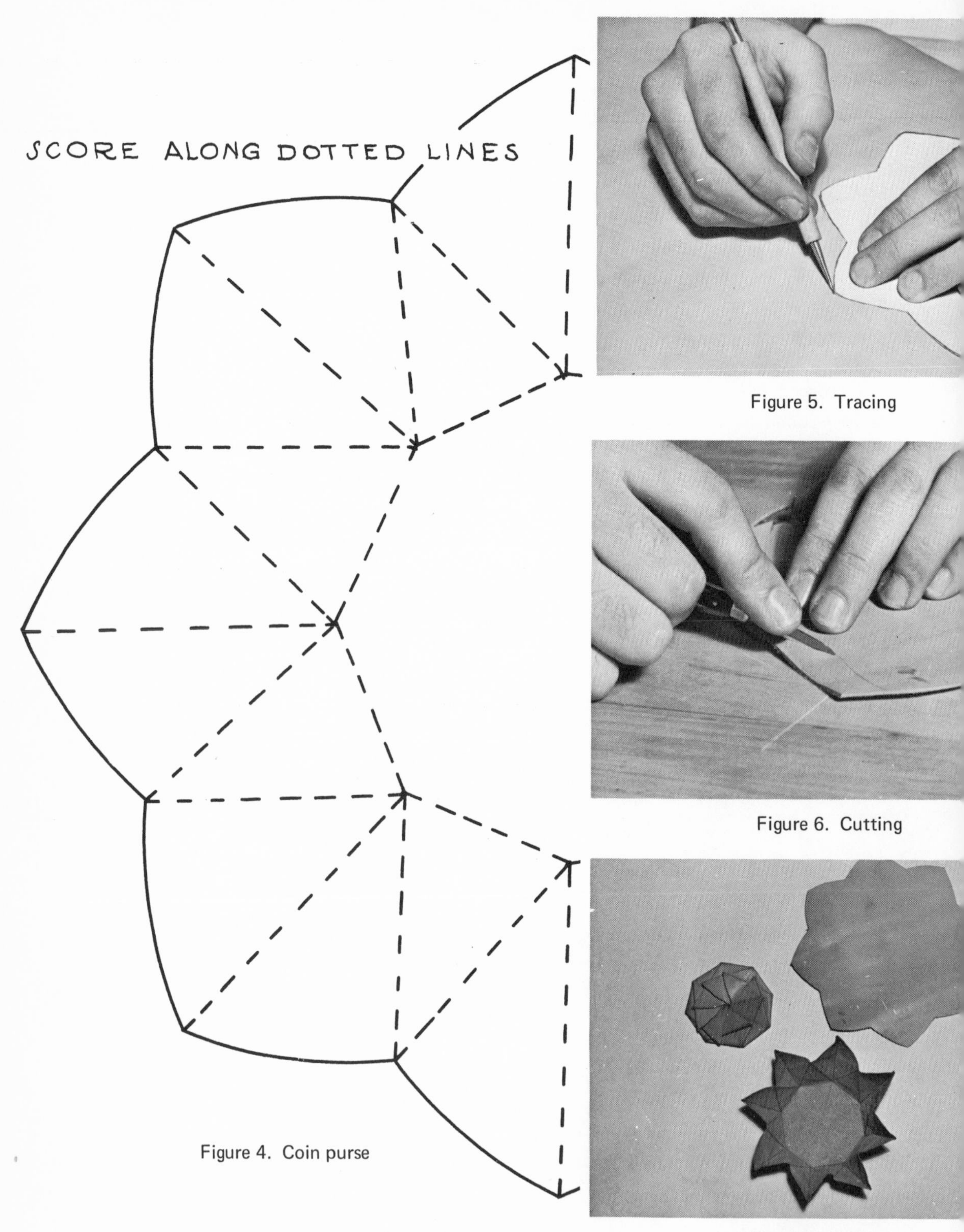

Figure 4. Coin purse

Figure 5. Tracing

Figure 6. Cutting

Figure 7. Folding

PROJECT 1: COIN PURSE *(Figure 4)*

1. The functional design, the size and shape of the coin purse are determined by the place in which it is to be carried.
2. Make a full-sized pattern that can be used for a layout. Use heavy paper. Try the pattern to see if the size and shape are suitable. *(Figure 4)*
3. Select leather which is toolable, such as tooling calfskin.
4. Prepare the leather for tooling by sponging it with clean water for a few minutes. This softens the leather and makes it pliable. Be sure to dampen the entire surface.
5. Transfer the pattern and/or the design by going over the lines on the pattern with an instrument such as a pencil or skewer. Before transferring, position the paper pattern in several places so as to utilize the leather with economy. *(Figure 5)*
6. Using the pattern, cut out the leather shape with a sharp knife or scissors. *(Figure 6)*
7. Using the modeling tool and a steel rule, press a line from the dots to where the arcs meet. Fold along these lines. Place between two clean sheets of paper, stand books on top, and allow to dry overnight. *(Figure 7)*
8. To clean and polish the leather, saddle soap is good. It is a mild cleaner as well as a finish for leather. Soap should be applied with a damp sponge and rubbed well into the leather with a circular motion. Polish with a soft cloth or lambskin when dry. Oxalic acid may be used for cleaning stubborn spots before applying the finish.

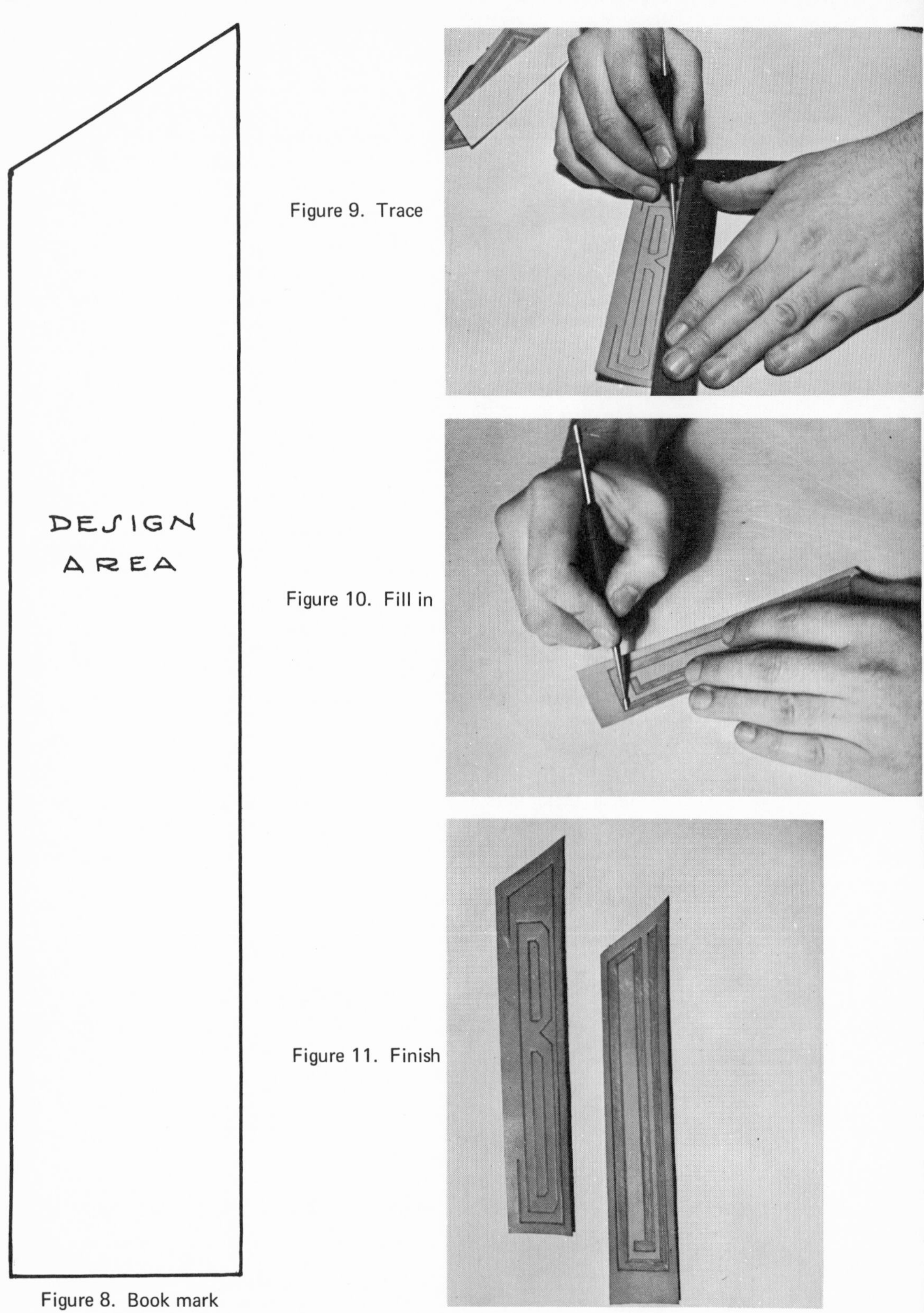

Figure 9. Trace

Figure 10. Fill in

Figure 11. Finish

Figure 8. Book mark

PROJECT 2: BOOKMARK *(Figure 8)*

1. Follow the same procedure as the previous project through step 6. Think in terms of straight lines, geometric shapes, and simple curved figures for your design.
2. Remove the pattern and dampen the surface of the leather. Sharpen the lines of the pattern by retracing several times, increasing the pressure until the design is very clear and the lines are depressed uniformly. This should be done on a fairly soft surface such as on top of a magazine. *(Figures 9, 10 and 11)*
3. Clean the leather as in Project 1 no. 8.

Figure 13. Transfer design

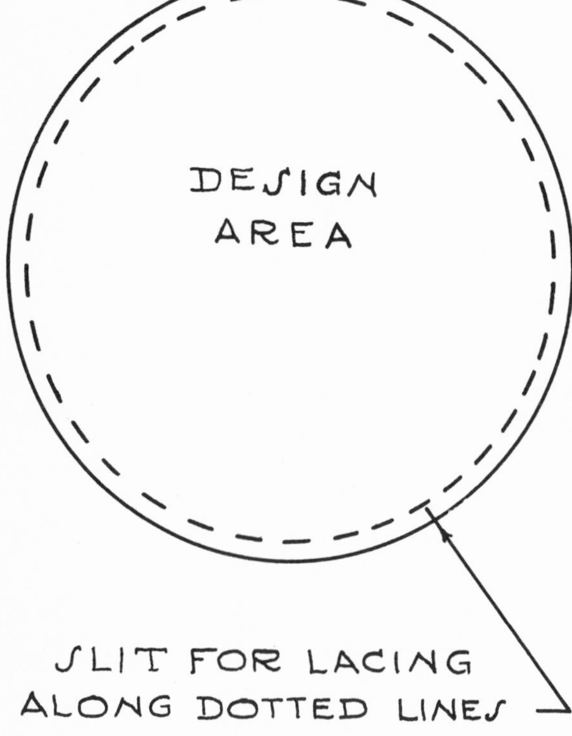

Figure 12. Coaster

Figure 14. Tap slits

Figure 15. Finished coaster

PROJECT 3: COASTER *(Figure 15)*

1. Follow the procedure for leather in the former projects through the first steps. The design should be made large enough to allow for lacing and to hold the container. Initials, overall patterned effects and texture are suggested for use.
2. Transfer the design. *(Figure 13)*
3. Tool as stated in the previous project.
4. Place the leather on a board and place a one-pronged thonging chisel about 1/8" in from the edge of the project. *(Figure 14)* A filed, 8 penny nail may be used for this process also. Tap with the mallet using enough force to cut through the leather. Continue making slits around the project. Slits should be placed about the width of one slit apart.
5. Lace with the type of stitch illustrated *(Figure 30)* which is the double-overlay or double buttonhole stitch. Variations of this stitch may also be used. Tuck loose ends under the stitching along the back side when finished lacing.
6. Even lace. Make lacing uniform by gently pounding with a mallet on the back side.
7. Clean and polish the leather as prescribed in earlier projects.

Figure 17. Punch holes top and bottom

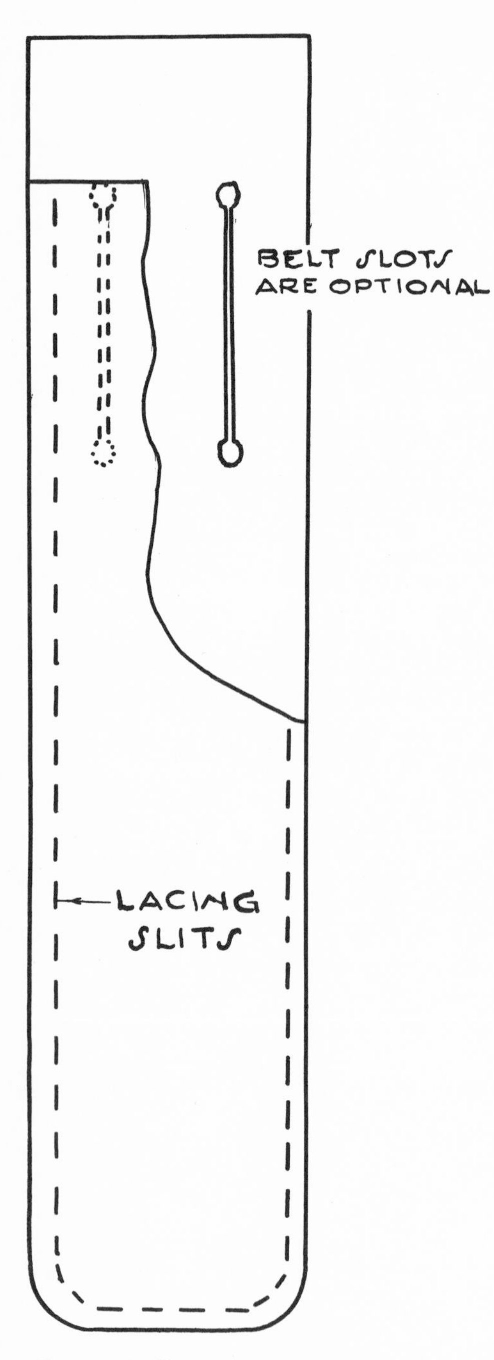

Figure 16. Pen and pencil pocket

Figure 18. Make slits

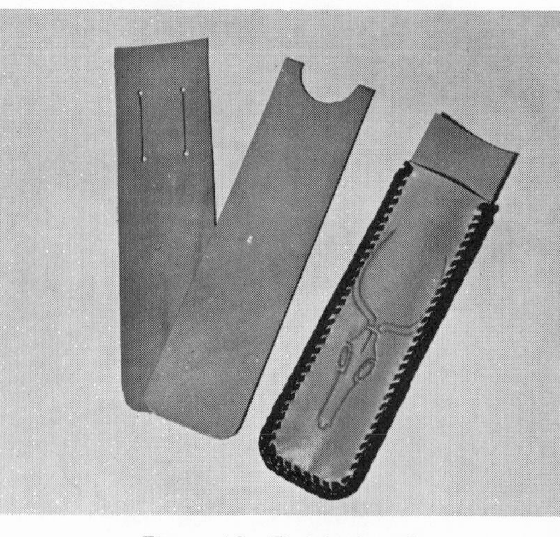

Figure 19. Finished project

PROJECT 4: PEN AND PENCIL POCKET
(Figure 16)

1. Prepare leather and design as outlined in previous projects and tool the design.
2. Punch a hole at the top and bottom of each slot. Cut a narrow slot from the top to the bottom hole about 1/16" wide (this step is optional). *(Figure 17)*
3. Apply a coat of rubber cement about ¼" on the project edges which are to be joined. Position the parts and allow them to dry.
4. All corners, which are to be laced, should be rounded with a dime or penny to facilitate a neat finished edge.
5. Place the leather on a board. Use the four-pronged thonging chisel along the straight edges and the one-prong chisel around the corners. There should be two slits in each corner. A filed, 8–penny nail may also be used for this process. Tap with the mallet using enough force to cut through the leather. *(Figure 18)*
6. The type of stitch illustrated is the double-over *(Figure 30)* or double buttonhole stitch. Variations of this stitch may be used. Tuck loose ends under the stitching along the back side when finished lacing.
7. Clean the finished piece as previously outlined. Finished project *Figure 19.*

PROJECT 5: KEY CASE *(Figure 20)*

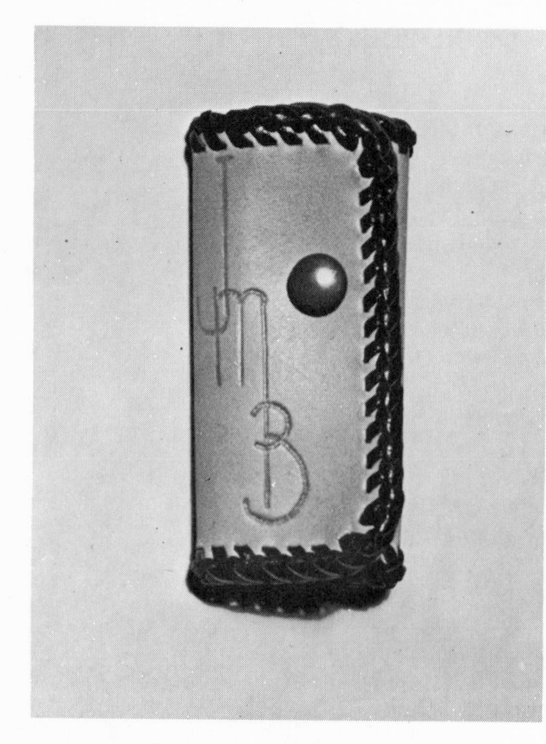

Figure 20. Leather key case

1. Prepare leather as outlined in previous projects. A monogram might be used for design here.
2. After you have designed, cut out the leather and tooled your design, clean the leather with saddle soap.
3. Use the modeler on the flesh side and score the leather at the folds to aid in folding the flaps.
4. Position the tongue of the case and cement the two pieces together at the point of lacing. Cement flesh side to flesh side.
5. Round the corners which are to be laced with a dime.
6. Make thonging slits 1/8" from the edges on all sides of the large piece. Use the one-and four-pronged thonging chisels for this operation.
7. Start with a piece of 3/32" goatskin lacing about 3" in length. To lace use the double overlay stitch. To splice refer to *Figure 30,* step 10.
8. Position the plate on the tongue and mark holes with a tracer. Punch holes with a revolving punch. Be sure to use the right size. Check the correct size by aligning the rivet with the proper tube on the revolving punch. *(Figure 22)*
9. Set the key plate to the tongue with rivets. *Make sure that the plate is right side up. (Figure 23)*
10. Use a snap setting tool. Punch the cap hole of the snap button. Then fold, mark, and punch the post ends of the snap button. *(Figure 24)*
11. Even the lacing by gently pounding with a mallet and board.

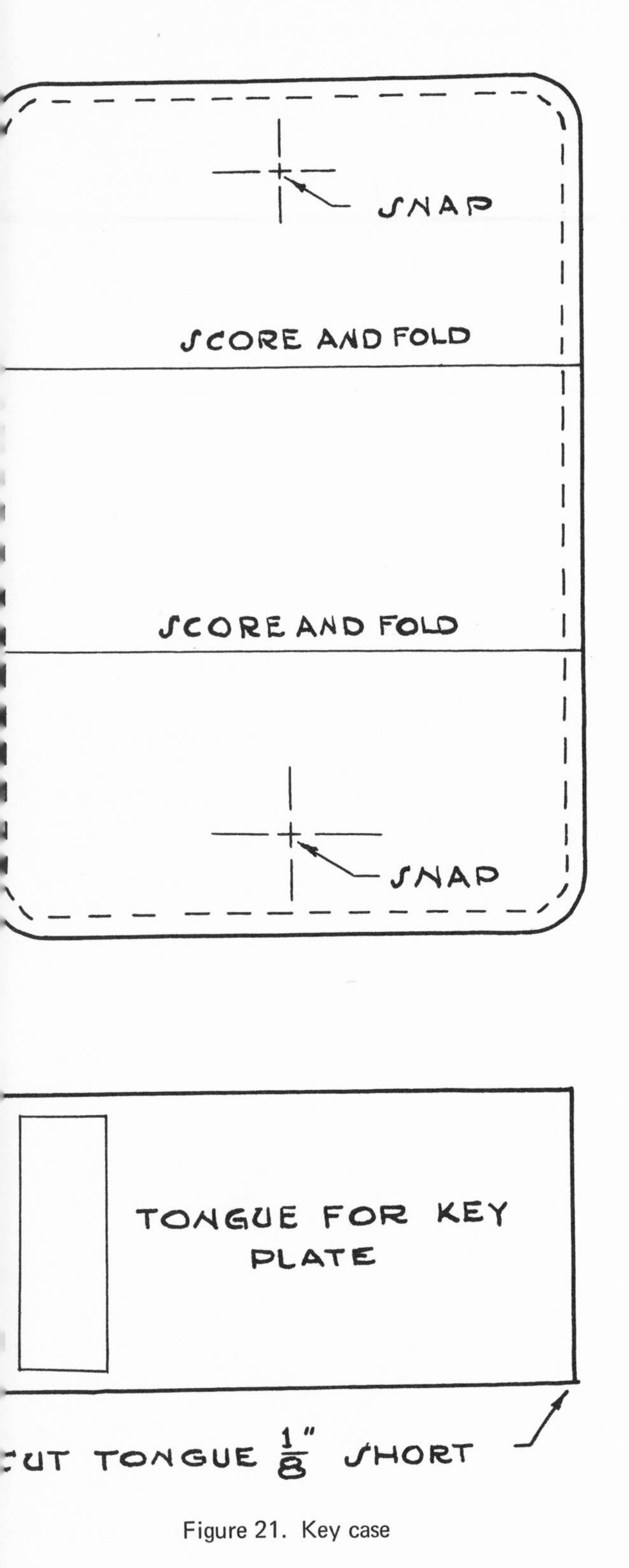

Figure 21. Key case

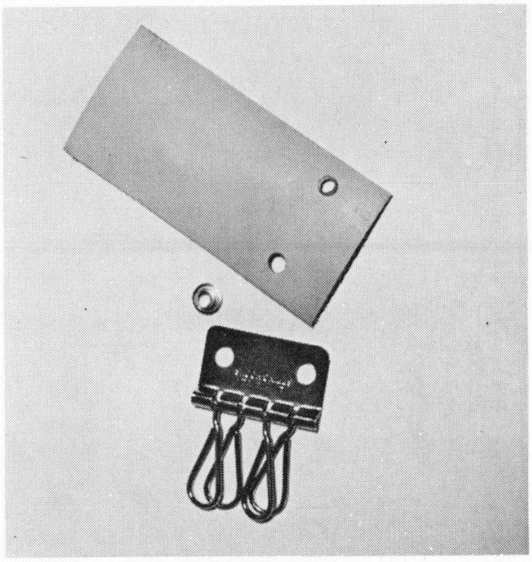

Figure 22. Mark holes

Figure 23. Set plate

Figure 24. Punch

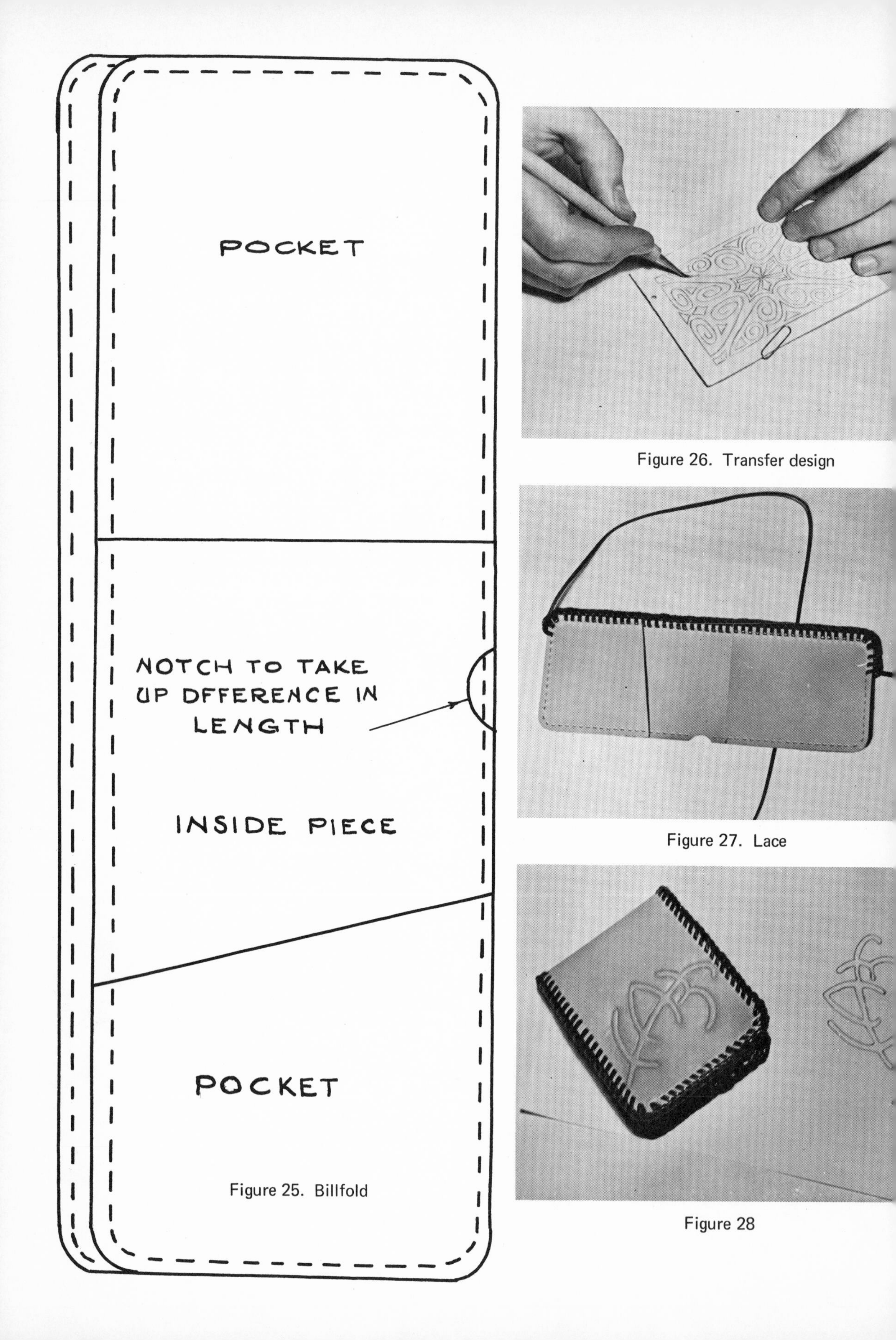

Figure 25. Billfold

Figure 26. Transfer design

Figure 27. Lace

Figure 28

PROJECT 6: LEATHER BILLFOLD

(Figure 28) Design *Figure 25*

1. Prepare the leather and the design.
2. Transfer the design. *(Figure 26)*
3. Tool and model the design.
4. Cut out an opening for a window. (Optional)
5. Cement the pockets to the center piece.
6. Place the leather on a cutting board. Use the four-pronged thonging chisel along straight edges and the one-prong chisel around the corners. A filed, 8–penny nail may be used for this process also. Tap with the mallet using enough force to cut through the leather.
7. Start lacing at the middle left end of the inside piece, cementing the end of the lace to the inside of the center piece. Lace across the pockets. Do not cut off the lace which is left over because you will continue lacing around the billfold as soon as you assemble it and make thong slits. *(Figure 27)*
8. Cement the edges of the assembled inside part to the edges of the cover, being sure not to cement the top edge.
9. Round the remaining corners and make thong slits 1/8" from the edge. All corners should be rounded with a dime or penny to facilitate a neat finished edge.
10. Continue lacing around the billfold. *(Figure 29)*
11. Clean and polish the leather.

Figure 30 shows the steps in lacing the double overlay stitch.

The preceding were a few suggestions for making articles in leather. Now that you have performed the steps, they should be easy. Experiment with the methods of applying design.

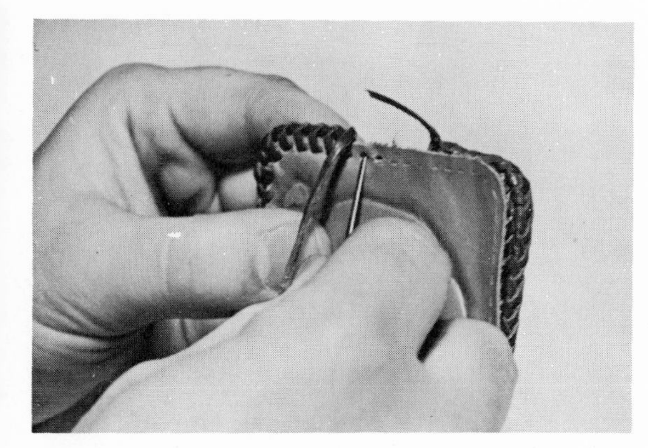

Figure 29. Continue lacing

Figure 30. Steps in lacing the double overlay stitch

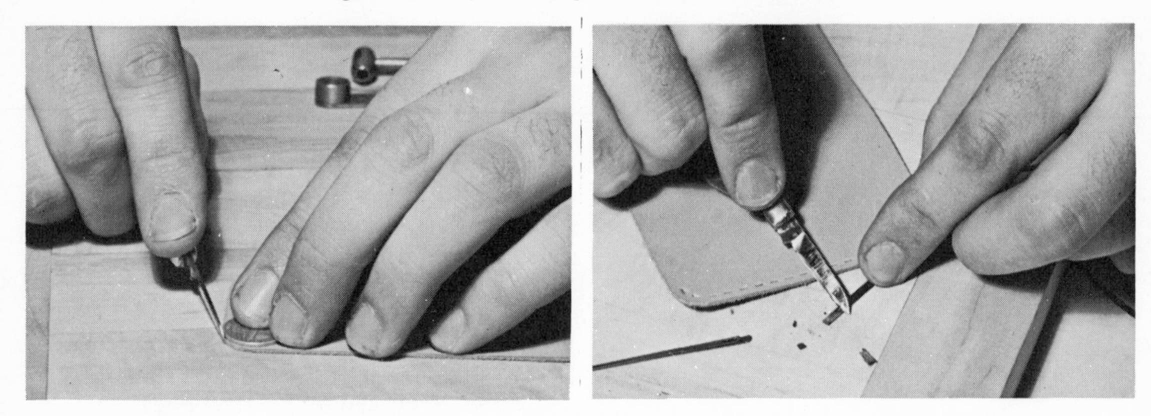

(1) Round corners to be laced

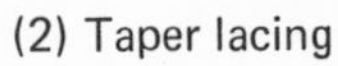

(2) Taper lacing

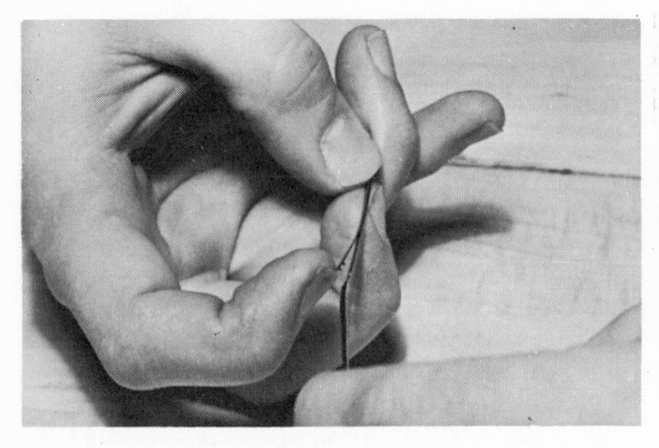

(3) Slip lace into needle

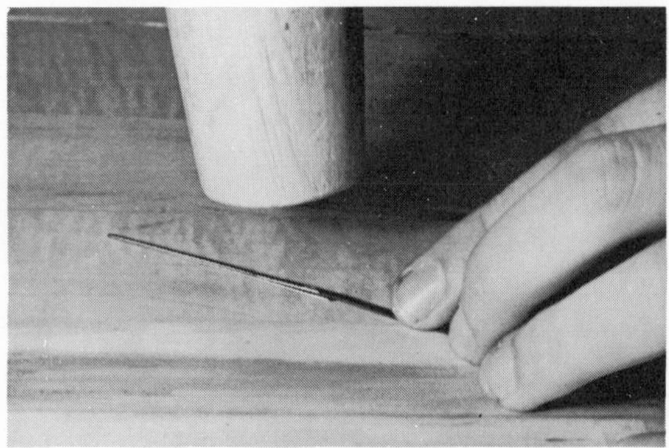

(4) Tap lightly

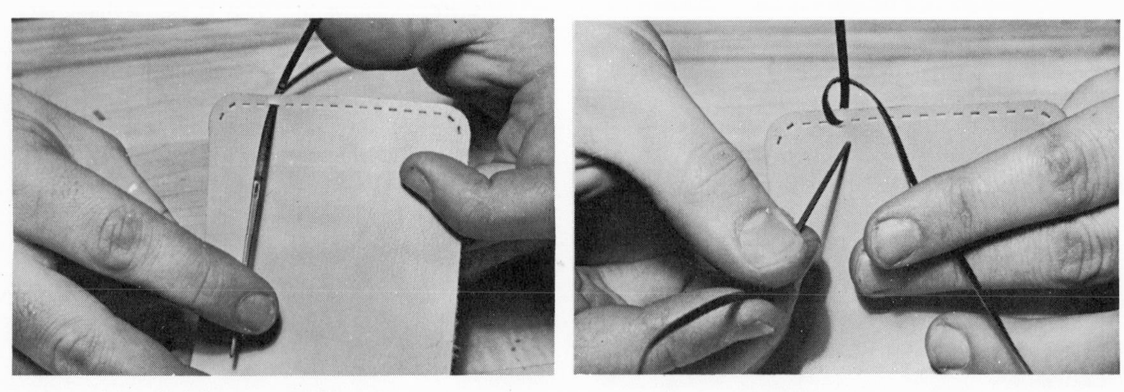

(5) Lace through slit

(6) Loop around lace

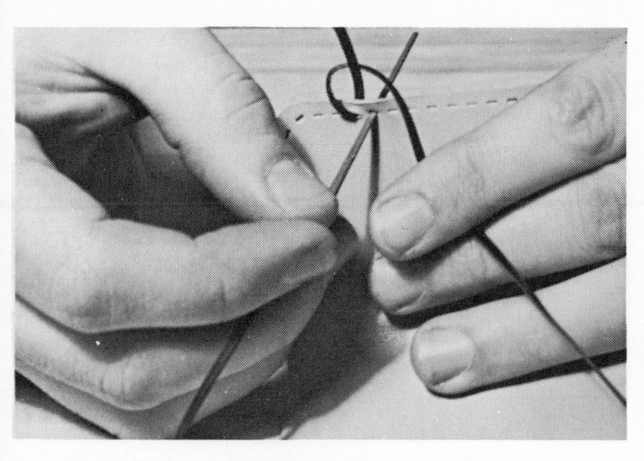

(7) Enter next slit from front side

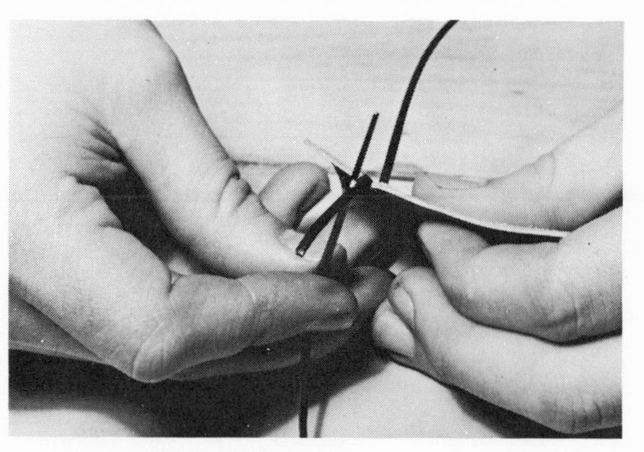

(8) Stitch under crossed strands from front

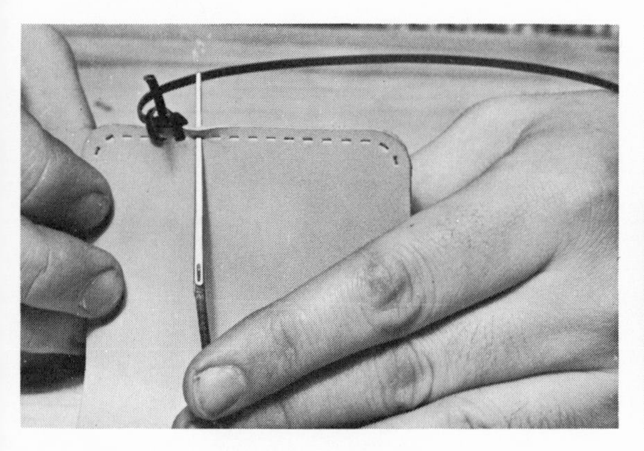

(9) Enter next slit and repeat last two steps

(10) Splicing with rubber cement

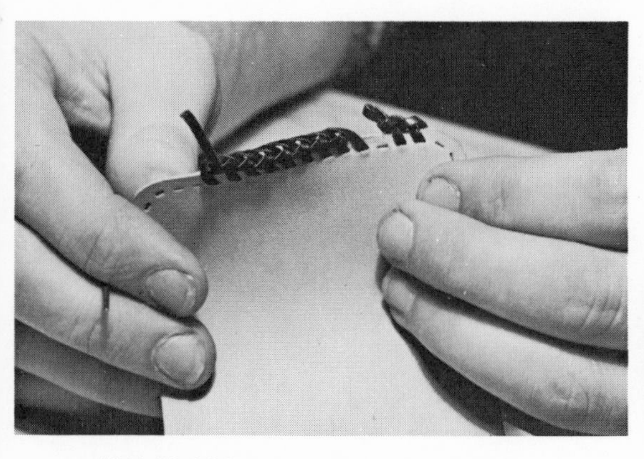

(11) Finishing up, remove first stitch

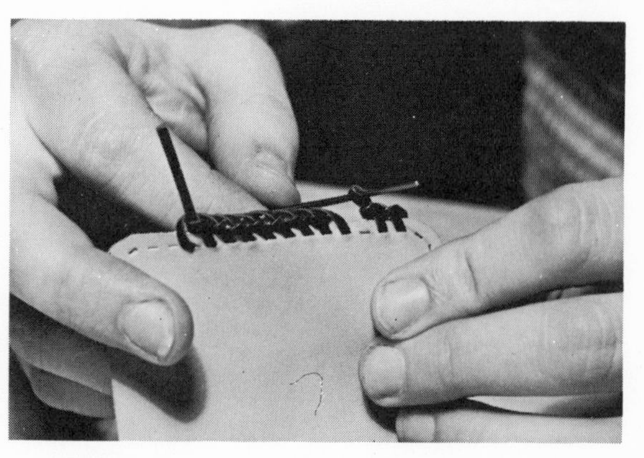

(12) Thread up through loop and under crossed strands

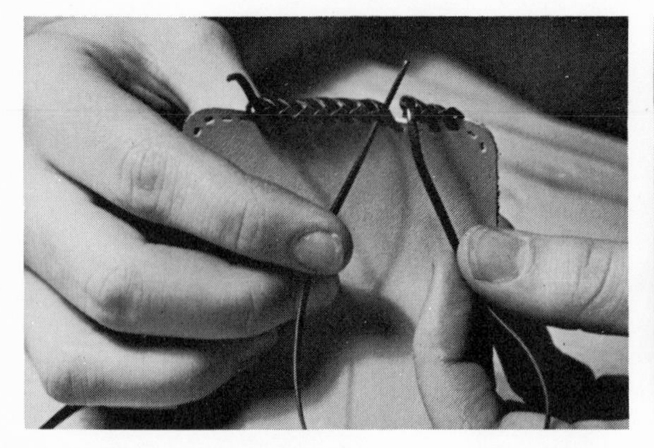

(13) Thread down through loop and into remaining slit

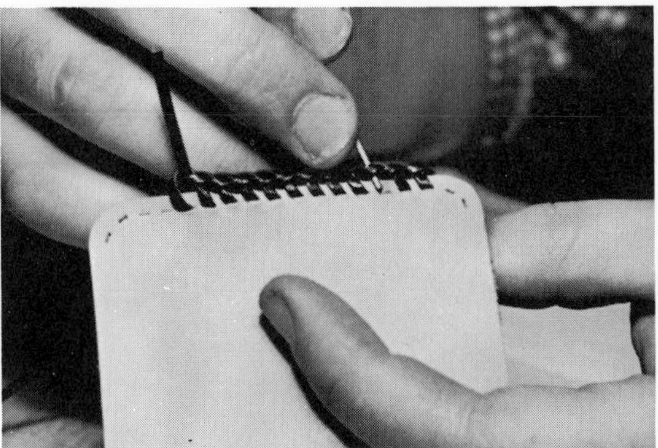

(14) Pull ends between pieces and cement to inside. Tap lacing uniformly flat with a mallet

MOSAICS

Materials needed:

Basics

- a form on which to apply the mosaic — tempered masonite is a good flat form; flower pots, boxes, trivettes, and other items can also be used
- tile-vinyl, rubber, glass or ceramic, wood pieces, seeds, stones
- white glue (white glue turns transparent when dry); Fuller's or Elmer's is suggested
- grout (mortar comes in white but can be dyed)
- design or idea
- saw
- scissors
- rags
- carbon or graphite paper

Extras

- cutting tool for glass and ceramic tile
- polish, such as floor wax
- plates, bowls, boxes, planters, and other full-round objects
- forms on which to place the tile
- metal frame for trivettes
- wood for frames, handles, and other parts of a functional object
- hammer and nails

Figure 1. War Memorial Facade, Milwaukee, Wisconsin, Edmund D. Lewandowski

Another craft which has been popular throughout history, practiced as early as the third millennium, B.C., especially in religious art, is mosaics. It is a craft which has absorbed the interest of participants and observers alike. Like all crafts, it ranges from the simple to more complex. It entails the combining of small bits of colored materials into a whole composition. Little children tear tiny pieces of colored paper and paste them to another paper to form a design or picture. They have even dyed small pieces of egg shells and pasted them onto a back board to make a colorful mosaic design. The craft progresses to the expert, "super" products of master craftsmen in the field, such as that shown in *Figure 1* of the beautiful mosaic on the facade of the War Memorial Building in Milwaukee, Wisconsin, by Edmund D. Lewandowski.

Mosaics have been used through the ages to improve the quality of a surface as well as to add strength to a weak surface. It was popular with the Mesopotamia builders, the Greeks, the Romans, the Early Christians, and the Renaissance artisans, as well as modern craftsmen. Although the simple mosaic of paper or egg shell is common, complicated materials such as red and black stone with white shell, colored marbles, glass, and thin sheets of gold have often been used. This craft is not only practical, but it is fun to do. It is easy. The technique is simple.

A design (often called the cartoon) is drawn on the surface to be decorated, and each small piece of material (often called "Tessera," from the Latin word meaning square piece) is glued on one at a time. Because this is so simple, it becomes a highly satisfactory leisure time activity. It also can be a social pastime; families may make mosaics as a team; entire school classes enjoy this project.

PROJECT 1: TILE FOR HOLDING HOT DISHES (using floor tile – *Figure 2*)

1. Cut a piece of tempered masonite 5" x 5" or larger. Masonite must be cut with a saw. Give the masonite a thorough coat of shellac or other sealer.
2. Cut pieces of colored vinyl tile exactly 1" square. These tiles may be cut with scissors. Beginners usually work with square pieces. Advanced students find more challenge in using odd shaped pieces.
3. Place these little squares on the masonite as in *Figure 3*; adjust them until you arrive at a pleasant design. Leave about 1/8" space between the tiles.
4. Glue these pieces down, using white glue which turns transparent when dry. Press this under a weight until the glue is dry and set. You may or may not apply grout to the spaces between the tiles. The first example, *Figure 2*, shows a simple mosaic without grout. Grouting is described at the end of this chapter.

Figure 2. Simple tile for holding hot dish

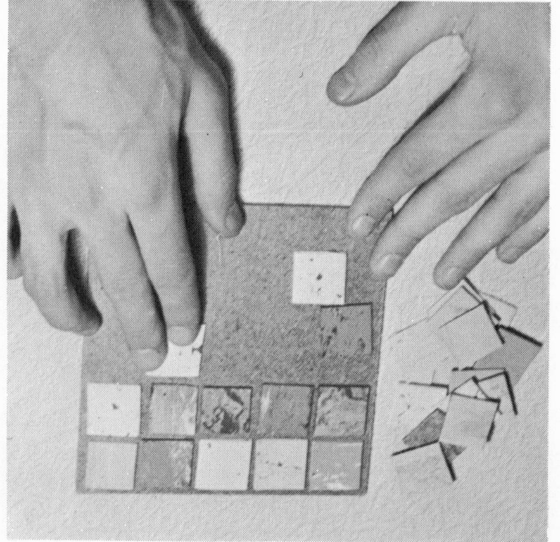

Figure 3. Place square tile pieces on shellaced masonite

PROJECT 2: TRIVETTE, USING CERAMIC TILE *(Figure 4)*

1. It is necessary to buy a trivette form for the base of the tile.
2. Instead of using vinyl tile as in Project 1, try ceramic tile. For variation and challenge instead of using square tiles, break up the ceramic tiles by placing them in a cloth bag and tapping lightly with a hammer. Ceramic and glass tiles may be cut with a cutting tool, but this tool is rather expensive.
3. Draw your design or form your plan for tile placement. You may adjust the tiles until the color plan satisfies you. Glue the tiles to the surface. Placing the pieces of tile on the trivette surface is like putting a jigsaw puzzle together. It may be so fascinating you will not want to leave it. Picture or pure design can be achieved. Try to get a balance and rhythm in the placement of your shapes and colors.
4. Grout. (See the end of this chapter.)

Figure 4. Trivette

PROJECT 3: DOOR STOP *(Figure 5)*

1. The base of this door stop is a plain flat brick, obtainable at brick yards. Be sure the brick is clean.
2. The bricks are covered with vinyl or rubber tile. Plain squares may be used as in the preceding project. *(Figure 5)* Better still, make all sides but one plain. Make the remaining side of odd-shaped pieces, as in *Figure 6.*
3. Plan your color scheme and arrangement of design. Glue the tiles.
4. Grout. (See the end of this chapter.)

Figure 6. Odd shapes are used for more of a challenge.

Figure 5. Door stop

PROJECT 4: BOOK ENDS *(Figure 7)*

1. The base of this project is brick also. This project is almost exactly like Project 3, except that the brick is sawed in half. Most brick yards have electric saws which will do the cutting.
2. Arrange the tile (the tiles shown are vinyl). Tiles may be square, as in the figure, or cut into odd shapes and arranged like a jig-saw puzzle. You might place felt or cork instead of tile on the bottom of the brick.
3. Glue the tiles.
4. Grout. (See the end of this chapter.)

Figure 7. Book ends

PROJECT 5: TRAY *(Figure 8)*

1. On a piece of tempered masonite 12" x 18", glue and nail wood trim, such as a piece of quarter round. Miter the corners. Two extra pieces glued and nailed to the 12" ends form the tray handles.
2. Design your picture on a 12" x 18" paper. Plan your colors.
3. Trace to transfer the design to the masonite.
4. Cut the vinyl tile in small pieces. Other tile such as glass, ceramic, or wood may well be used.
5. Fit and glue the tile to the masonite to form your picture. In *Figure 8* a piece of copper wire was glued to the masonite to form the fish shape before the tile was applied. For a tray, mortar or grout between tile pieces is necessary for functional use and the cleaning of the tray. Apply grout as described at the end of this chapter.
6. Finish by polishing the tile.
7. Paint with enamel or varnish or stain and varnish the wood trim.

Figure 8. Tray

Figure 9. Mosaic picture

Figure 10. Place grout directly on tiles and fill in spaces

Figure 11. Wipe off excess grout. Polish.

PROJECT 6: MOSAIC PICTURE *(Figure 9)*

1. Use a piece of tempered masonite the size you want for your picture. Smaller ones may be about 9" x 12"; larger, 12" x 15" or 12" x 18".
2. Draw your picture the correct size. If your design is too small, enlarge it in the following fashion:

   Block off your small picture in half and half again horizontally and vertically. On a paper the size you want your picture, do the same. Look at the original and follow the lines of the picture by watching squares. Pictures may be held horizontally or vertically or may be square. Pictures may be diminished in the same manner.
3. Trace your picture (now the correct size) onto your masonite. Use carbon paper or graphite paper.
4. Apply tiles by placing them according to your plan. Arrange them until the design and color please you, then glue.
5. Grout. (See the end of this chapter.)
6. Finish by polishing and buffing.

   Variations and other projects are shown in *Figure 12.*

Grout is a substance much like plaster-of-paris, but it hardens more slowly. Mix grout and water to the consistency of very heavy cream. Place this mixture directly on the tile and fill the spaces thoroughly. *(Figure 10)* Wipe off the excess. Allow it to set. Do not dry by artificial heat or blower. Clean by wiping with a damp cloth. Polish. *(Figure 11)* If rubber or vinyl tile is used, polish the surface with floor wax or a soft cloth. If glass or ceramic tile is used, polish with a dry soft cloth or an electric buffer.

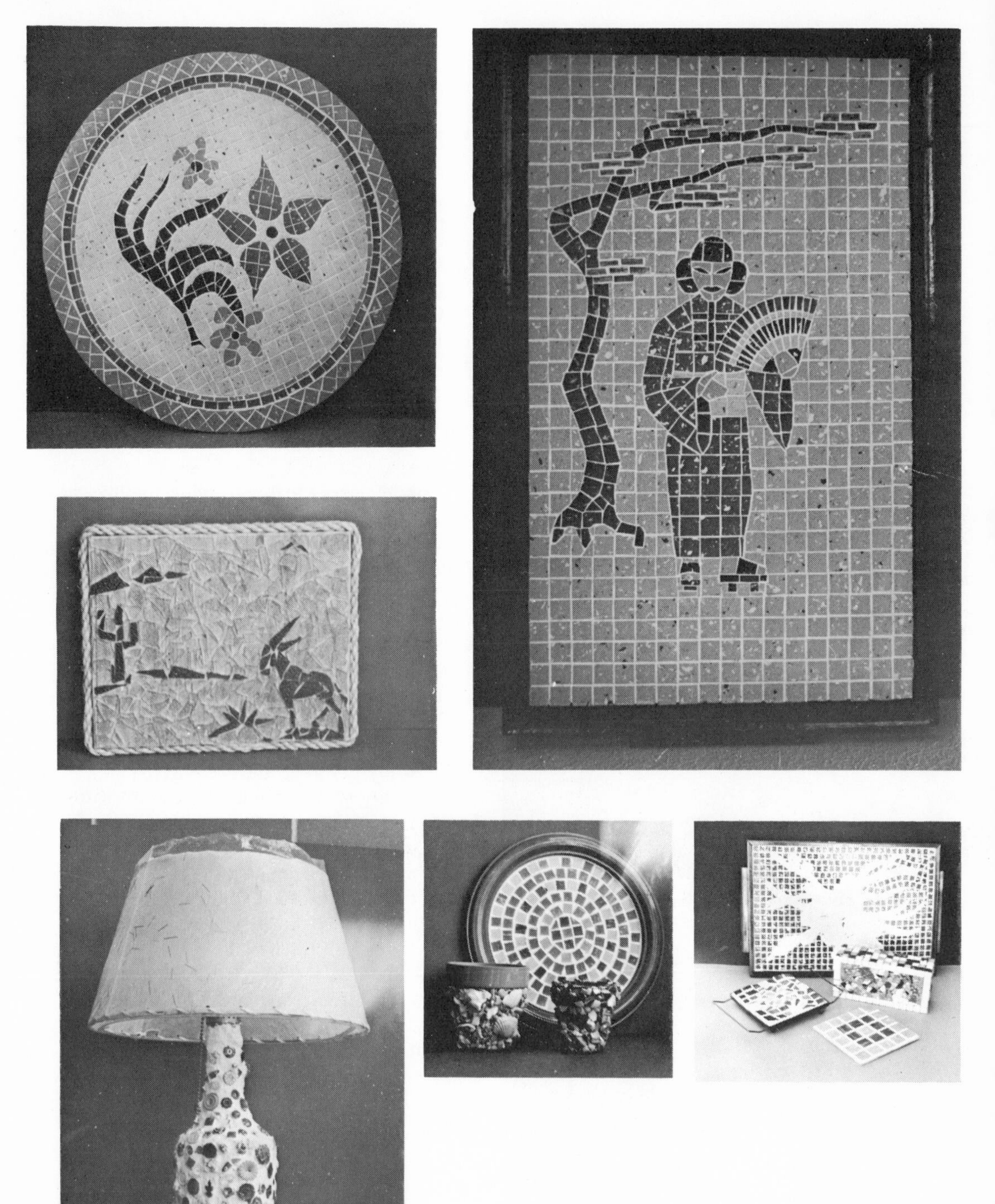

Figure 12. Variations and other projects

PAPER

Materials needed:

- Basics
  - paper
    - newspaper
    - paper towels
    - toweling
    - toilet or facial tissue
  - pencils
  - scissors
  - stapler
  - adhesives—wheat paste
  - string
  - paint (tempera)
  - paint brush
  - wire
- Extras
  - paper
    - tissue
    - crepe
    - unprinted news
    - brown wrapping
    - colored construction
    - corrugated
    - metallic
    - stencil papers
    - lace doilies
    - paper bags
    - egg and apple carton dividers
  - small knife
  - dull razor blade (single edge)
  - eraser
  - gum tape
  - compass
  - triangle
  - ruler
  - chicken wire
  - wood
  - balloons
  - odd materials
    - felt
    - foil
    - feathers
    - buttons
  - scrap materials
  - spray paint

Figure 1. This float was used for the Aquatennial Minnesota Centennial. The horses are paper, the girls are real! The basic form used was shredded paper and thread for the molding, finishing off with strips of paper and papier-maché. The final piece de resistance: gilding!

Paper has many uses. Generally, we think of it in terms of two dimensions and its uses for drawing and painting. However, its possibilities for construction and sculpture are tremendous.

Paper sculpturing and papier-mache may be simple as the little paper chains made by kindergartners for Christmas tree and room decorations, as interesting as the full round and relief masks, mobiles, and stage settings made by high school students, or as challenging as the great floats, such as those in the Mardi Gras parade in New Orleans, the Winter Carnival in Saint Paul, and the Aquatennial in Minneapolis.

There is a vast assortment of colors and types of papers which can be used. Rough and smooth papers, corrugated, cellophane, tissue, construction, metallic foils, newspaper, lace doilies, and shelf paper are some of the papers used in paper construction. Paper projects are suited to many occasions. Usually, basic paper crafts are finished with paint, cloth, and other decorative items.

The craft of paper construction is an inexpensive one. If it is done creatively, it will follow no definite rule since the processes vary with each exploration. To work without a preliminary drawing and rules may have distinct advantages because it may prove to be more creative. The materials themselves present the motivation. The direct approach avoids monotony and often presents more exciting results. However, several basic projects are suggested for a beginning.

Certain procedures which require practice and skill are often necessary to the production of finished samples. Many full and detailed books have been published on these directions, and they are listed in the bibliography. They involve such experiences as cutting, scoring, folding, curling, rolling, pressing into place, building from a base, fastening and joining, making shapes–cylinders, cones, triangles, circles, and squares–making paper stand, making some parts stick out, and constructing an armature.

As few directions as possible should be given and a few basic ideas presented. The materials together with inspiration will do the rest. These basic understandings are necessary in the execution of most paper sculpture and mache.

The finished projects are abstractions, and one can abstract ideas from almost everywhere. Study, observe and think about birds, animals, and other forms of nature, and you will find shapes, forms, and color for the characteristics you wish to express. (Naturally the forms will not be photographic in appearance.) They are often called "animuls" instead of animals.

Paper sculpture indicates the process and skill of paper rolling, bending, folding, cutting, tearing, pasting, and stapling together to make light sculptural forms. *(Figure 2)*

Papier-maché, on the other hand, is the French name for paper mash which means the shaping of paper pulp into more solid form to build shapes. The following is common to all papier-maché:

1. The work usually requires an armature, a skeletal framework of wire, newspaper, wood, or some similar strong framework securely fastened together.
2. The paste is made by sifting wheat paste (paper hanger's paste) slowly into water. Mix until soupy. Follow directions on the paste sack.
3. Most often strips about ½" wide and several inches long are soaked in the paste and applied to the armature in several layers. It is best to apply one layer and let it dry before applying the second. Three or four layers may be necessary.
4. Occasionally, pulp is used to give added body where needed. Pulp is made by tearing paper into small pieces, soaking the pieces in water, squeezing, and adding the paste mixture. Squeeze out excess paste, add to the form, and model almost as you would clay.
5. These forms should dry slowly from inside to out. Do not dry by artificial blower or heat.
6. The finish consists of painting, adding cloth, yarn, buttons, special paper, or any material suited to the desired result.

Figure 2. Paper sculpture

PROJECT 1: PAPER SCULPTURE

Relief paper sculpture *(Figure 3)*

1. Select a background paper about 12" x 18". Construction paper or tag board is good.
2. Out of a sheet of contrasting colored construction paper cut a basket, simple in shape, but symmetrical. Cut slits in the basket and weave strips of contrasting colored construction paper through these slits. Staple the basket to the background loosely so that it stands out from the background.
3. From old magazines, bits of scrap paper, cloth, or felt, design your flowers. Mount them at different levels. Use different colors. Let some of them hang down like vines. Construct them in three dimensions so that parts stand out from the background. Use your imagination. Fasten them to the basket and background with glue or staples.

Figure 3. Paper relief flowers in woven basket and relief character

Figure 4. Paper giraffe

Giraffe and Lion *(Figures 4, 5 and 6)*

The lion is similar to the giraffe except for the following additions:

1. The mane is made by folding a strip of brown paper (about 6" wide and 36" long) into an accordion fold. Slit the ends to give a fringed effect.
2. Staple the ends of the accordion together to form the circle.
3. Staple this accordion piece to the body in two or three places.
4. Cut the face any shape you like and allow the parts to protrude to make a three dimensional effect.
5. Staple the head to the accordion piece and through to the body.
6. Add tongue depressors to the inside of each of the four legs so the lion will stand.
7. Add thin paper strips, straws, or wire for the tail and whiskers.

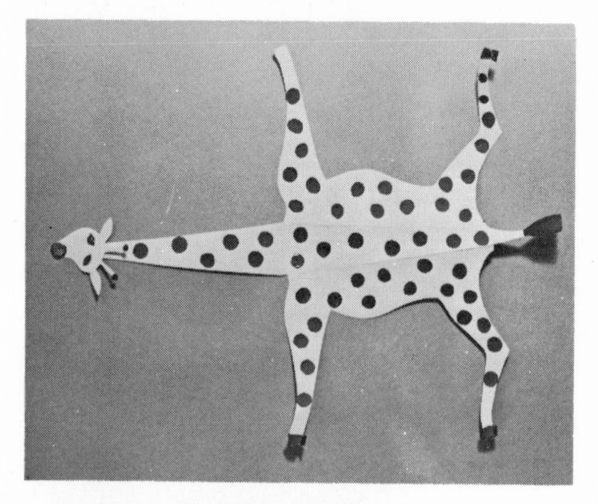

Figure 5. Paper giraffe - flat design

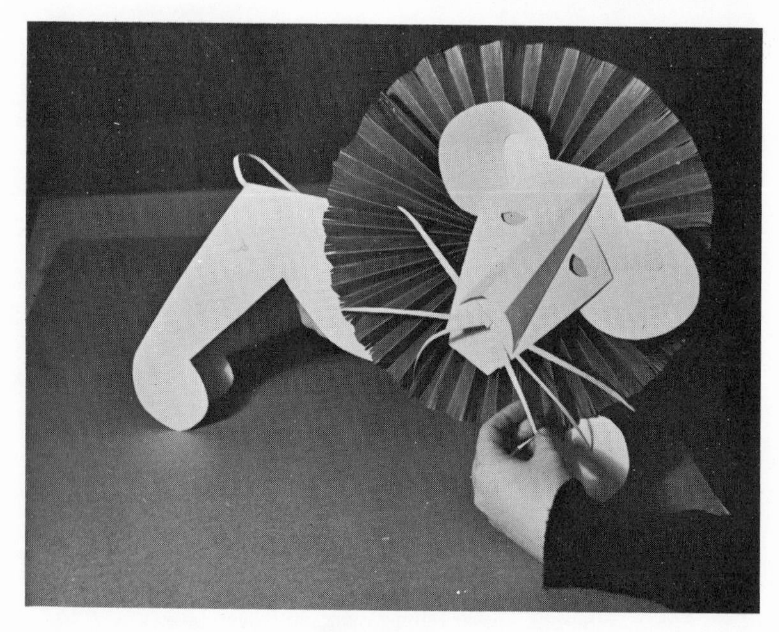

Figure 6. Lion

Figure 7. Crepe paper - sculptured clown

Figure 8. Paper sack clown

PROJECT 2: CLOWN *(Figure 7)*

Crepe Paper Sculptured Clown

1. With a double strength of stove pipe wire, or any similar wire, form the skeletal framework of a clown (back bone, legs, arms, head). For the size shown the body and legs require about 12" of double wire, the arms 6" of double wire.
2. To make the arms, form crepe paper over the wire loosely. Tie at the shoulder and stuff newspaper or tissue paper between the wire and the crepe paper. Tie the crepe paper at the wrist, leaving extra for a ruffle. Do the same for the other arm. Take another piece of crepe paper 12" x 15" and slit this up 5" for the legs. Form as you did the arms. Last, form the head like the rest of the clown.
3. Make the hands, feet, and hat out of construction paper or tag board.
4. Put hair, ruffles, tassels, and other trim on with crepe paper as in *Figure 7.*

Paper Sack Clown

Another variation of the paper clown is *Figure 8.*

1. Blow up four sacks, one for the head, one for the body, and two for the legs. Stuff these with paper.
2. Join these parts together with strings, thread, stapler, or paste.
3. Wind the bottom of the sack with crepe paper and attach the cardboards for a foot base.
4. Form the arms by the process of zig-zag. Zig-zag is done as follows: take two equal sized strips of paper and place them at right angles. Staple the ends together. Fold the bottom up over the top strip and continue (a over b, b over a). Repeat until desired length is reached. Always keep the folds at right angles. Attach this to the body with a stapler.
5. Make a hat out of crepe paper, gathered at the top and tasseled with more crepe paper strips.
6. Finish by painting the clown suit with tempera in a bright pattern. Add paint to the face. This object may now be hung or it may stand on its feet.

PROJECT 3: PAPIER-MACHÉ TURTLE
(Figure 9)

1. Fill two regular sized paper plates with newspaper and staple the edges together to form the turtle's body.
2. Fill a small paper bag with paper. Crumble it together and form some wire over it to form a head. Connect the head to the body with the wire by sliding it between the two paper plates.
3. Roll a piece of newspaper and form wire around it for the feet. Slide between the plates.
4. Insert a pipe cleaner or chenille-covered wire into the back between the plates to form a tail. Cover this with felt or crepe paper.
5. Apply papier-maché by wrapping the entire frame with layers of newspaper or tissue paper. The paper must be covered with paste and laid on in layers, allowing each layer to dry before another is added, until the desired thickness and durability is obtained.
6. Dry thoroughly.
7. Finish as follows:
   a. Paint the entire surface with green-darker for the body and lighter for the head and feet.
   b. Glue shell-shaped macaroni to the back of the turtle and paint it dark green. Do not paint the entire shell, however; this contrast gives a nice texture.
   c. Staple buttons on for eyes.
   d. Add green and red felt for the nose and toes.

Figure 9. Papier-maché turtle

PROJECT 4: PAPIER-MACHÉ BUNNY
(Figure 10)

1. With chicken wire form three balls of varying sizes – the largest 36" wide and 14" tall, the next 18" x 7", and the smallest 14" x 7".
2. Cut ears from chicken wire, approximately 9" long. Cut arms 20" long (folded over). Cut paws 8" long. Make each a 2" square.
3. Stuff the body, ears, arms, and paws with dry crumpled newspaper. This will give these parts firmness.
4. Connect all these units together with fine wire.
5. Place on heavy cardboard and secure with wire or staple to form your base.
6. Apply paste soaked strips to the entire form as described in the introduction. Add paper pulp to the cheeks to give bulk and form.
7. Dry thoroughly.
8. Paint the entire rabbit with white tempera or other white paint.
9. Apply shellac to sections with a brush or spray (beginning at the bottom) and immediately spray "sno-spray" or other textured material to this surface.
10. Cut out pink felt pieces and glue them on for the eyes, nose, and mouth.
11. Cut two thin pieces of styrofoam to form teeth. Glue these inside the mouth. Secure with pins.
12. Finish as follows:
    a. Punch an artificial flower into one hand.
    b. Cut grass-like strips of construction paper and attach to tagboard.
    c. Add a tail of wool yarn.

Figure 10. Papier-maché bunny

PROJECT 5: PAPIER-MACHÉ MOUSE
(Figure 11)

1. Make the frame out of wood, and form chicken wire around it to give the full-round appearance. Stuff it with crumpled paper.
2. Form the ears with wire. Attach to the head.
3. Cover the entire body with papier-maché (as described in the introduction) making necessary fullness with paper pulp. Form the feet at this time.
4. Wire the tail securely to the body and wind with papier-maché.
5. Dry thoroughly.
6. Attach black felt to the tail and inside of the ears and pink felt to the tips of the paws, eyes, and nose.
7. Using any type of fur-like material, paste on small pieces to cover the entire body.
8. Stick wire through the nose for whiskers. Cover with felt.

Figure 11. Papier-maché mouse

PROJECT 6: PAPIER-MACHÉ MASK
(Figure 12)

1. Form a frame of chicken wire over the head of a person. Shape it and fit it on to the shoulders where it will eventually rest. Be sure to leave plenty of breathing space. Wire the frame together securely.
2. Apply paste-soaked strips to this armature, or framework, as described in the introduction. Leave an opening in the mouth which will be your "vision" spot. You will find with a mask of this size that the mouth is about in line with your eyes.
3. Add the ears at this time. They may be paper attached to wire or merely heavy paper fastened to the head with staples. Papier-maché strips are applied to the ears and then to the head to give added security.
4. For special forms add paper pulp to jowels and lips where necessary for added fullness.
5. Pierce holes for the eyes and embed rubber balls into the papier-maché. A glass marble can be set into each of the rubber balls and glued securely.
6. Add a nose and teeth of styrofoam. Leave the teeth white. Paint the nose black.
7. Paint the lips and the inside of mouth dark red.
8. Paint the inside of the ears black.
9. Cover the entire remaining frame by pasting on flannel cloth with a leopard design. Insert colored pipe cleaners or chenille-covered wire through the hole for whiskers.

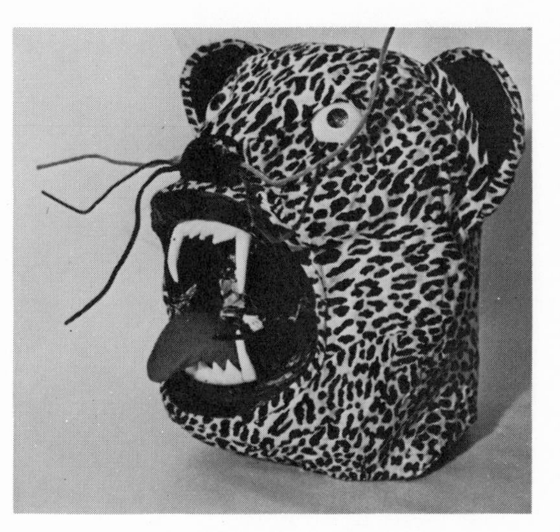

Figure 12. Papier-maché mask

Other figures show more papier-maché projects. *Figure 13*, an elephant; *Figure 14*, a clown; *Figure 15*, a poodle; *Figure 16*, a snake; *Figure 17*, a seal; *Figure 18*, a crooked man; and *Figure 19*; a puppet.

Paper sculpture and papier-maché projects have been suggested. The last picture is a true Mexican pinata which is also made of papier-maché. *(Figure 20)* It is a figure which is used in the celebration of Mexican festivals, particularly at Christmas time. The inside of the form is filled with candies and surprises, and the form is suspended from the ceiling. Someone is selected, blindfolded, and turned around three times. With a stick the blindfolded person strikes at the suspended form to break it. The surprises fall out into the hands of other people gathered around. This is a national ceremony.

It is important to leave the pinata hollow inside when making it. You can create this hollow by building the body over a balloon, using it as a mold. Wrap four or five layers of paper strips dipped in paste and water over and around the blown-up balloon. When the paper strips are dry remove the balloon by piercing it. Fill the body with candies and presents and build on the other parts of it after it has been sealed. After the other parts are secured, decorate the form by painting or covering it with brightly colored tissue paper which you can shred or curl.

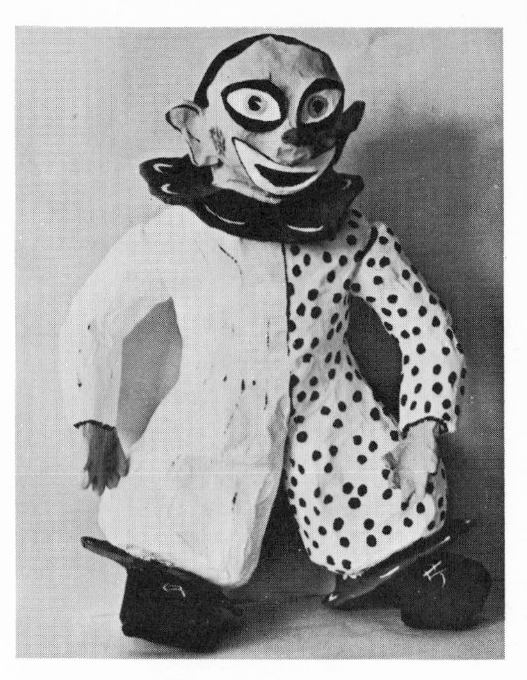

Figure 14. Clown

Figure 13. Elephant

Figure 15. Poodles

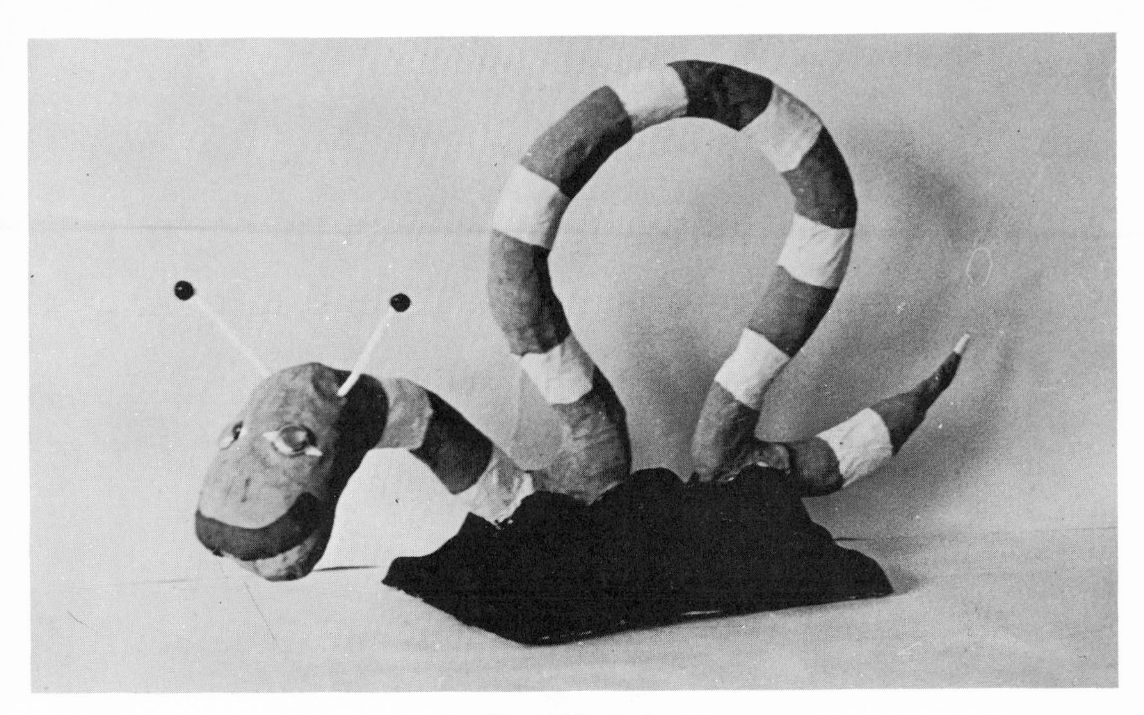

Figure 16. Snake

Figure 17. Seal

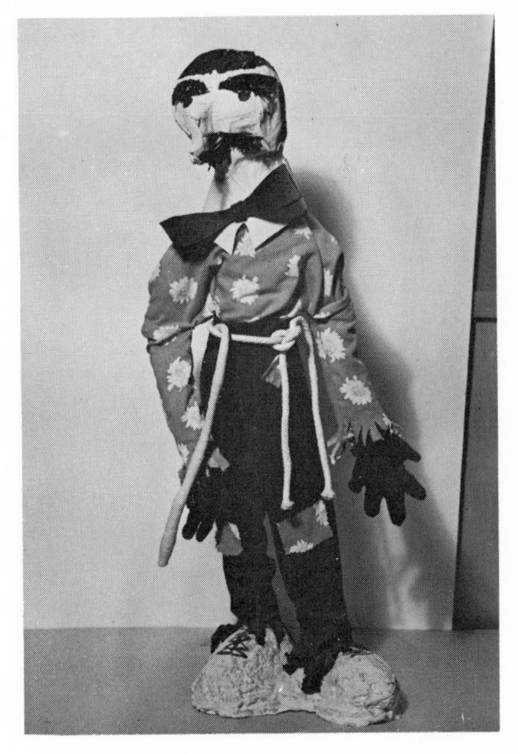

Figure 18. Crooked man

Figure 19. Mexican puppet

Figure 20. Mexican piñata

PLASTICS

Materials needed:

Basics

- liquid plastic (clear casting resin)
- mold release
- catalyst
- mold of some type
- embeddments of some type
- paper cups for mixing (4 oz. cups are recommended)
- sticks for stirring

Extras

- fancy molds (original shapes)
- fancy embeddments
- jewelry findings
- coloring agent
- surface hardener
- oil base clay
- white glue or airplane glue

Plastics, as presented in this chapter, is a relatively new medium in the field of crafts. Its use in industry, however, has been widespread in recent years, for example: plastic has been used in the automotive industry; in furniture and interior design; for modern kitchen appliances and utensils; in clothing manufacturing; sporting goods; architecture; fine appointments and jewelry; and a variety of other fields. The possibilities for future use of this craft continue to amaze the experts. The vast scope and steady growth of this "miracle medium" presents a challenge to both the professional designer and the novice. The evidences of this new material are apparent and visible daily, and it is not uncommon for one to be baffled by the use and results of plastics. Often we see a plastic imitation of stone and wood. This is not its intended use, however, for this material has a characteristic unique to itself. In its basic use plastics is a wonderful new discovery and contribution to science, industry, and aesthetic art. Durability, strength, flexibility, simplicity, and versatility are but a few of its characteristics.

It is the intention of this writer to interest and stimulate the reader, both in current industrial projects and in plastics as a craft. As you observe the commercial use of plastics and participate in the following suggested craft projects, you will become familiar with and may be inspired by the possibilities of this new medium. Materials needed *(Figure 1)*

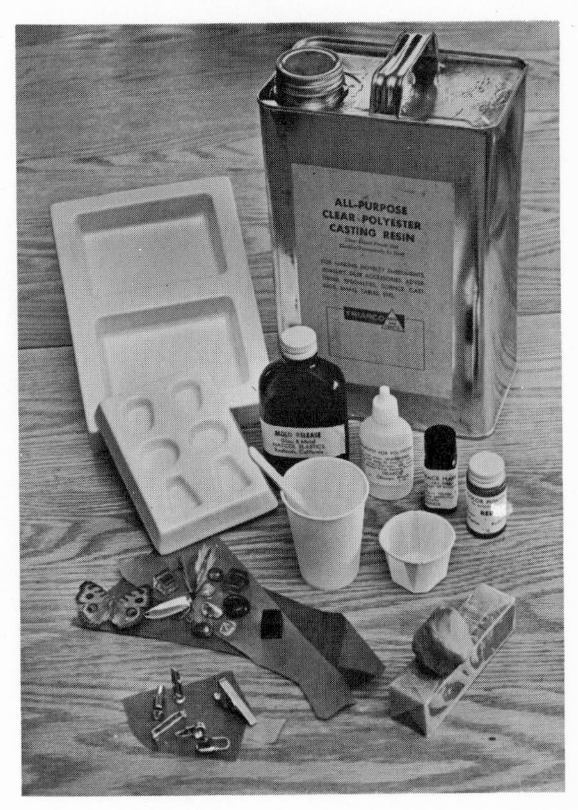

Figure 1. Materials needed

PROJECT 1: SIMPLE PLASTIC PLACQUE WITH EMBEDDMENTS *(Figure 2)*

1. Use a clean coffee can cover (preferably the plastic type).
2. If the cover is not the plastic type, cover thoroughly with mold release. With a plastic cover no mold release is necessary because the hardened piece will pop out from the cover.
3. Put the cover on a flat, stable surface so that the plastic will be level when poured in.
4. Lay the embeddments in the cover. Anything which is dry may be embedded. The embeddments should not exceed the thickness of the cover.
5. Mix the plastic. The plastic used for this project is "All Purpose Clear Polyester Cooking Resin." One oz. liquid plastic and 8–10 drops of catalyst should be used. Stir thoroughly and it is ready to pour. The more catalyst used, the faster the hardening process. It is always desirable to work in a room temperature of approximately 70° F.
6. Pour this mixture over the embeddments in the cover. Spread so that all the area is covered.
7. Leave the cover until the plastic has set and is hard.
8. Remove from the mold. If you have difficulty getting the plastic out of the mold after it has hardened, place it in a cool place (deep freeze) over night. This causes it to contract and to come out of the mold easily.
9. The finished project may be used as a wall plaque by attaching a hanger to the back.

Figure 2. Simple plastic plaque with embeddments

PROJECT 2: JEWEL TRIVET *(Figure 3)*

1. Into a commercial trivet form, pour the plastic mixture (½ oz. liquid plastic to 4–5 drops of catalyst stirred thoroughly). Spread evenly to all edges and corners so the entire trivet is covered.
2. Place colored marble jewels in the trivet according to your desired design. This should be done quickly before the plastic dries. (The thinner the layer of plastic, the quicker it will dry.)
3. Allow to dry thoroughly and set.

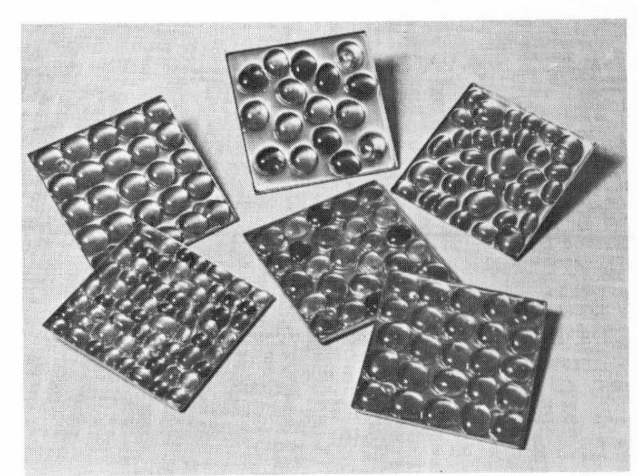

Figure 3. Jewel trivet

PROJECT 3: JEWELRY *(Figure 4)*

1. Molds for simple jewelry are available at craft stores. (You may form your own by using oil base clay.)
2. Paint mold release in each mold to be used.
3. Pour a very thin layer of plastic into the mold. This will form a protective top coat for your piece of jewelry. Remember, the bottom of your mold is the top surface of the jewelry. (The mold is turned upside down to release the contents.)
4. Put the desired embeddments into these molds. Fish flies, shells, starfish, seahorses, pieces of gimp, dried flowers, and other dry articles may be used. Put these embeddments in the molds upside down, so when they come out they will be reversed.
5. Mix plastic in the cup, 1 oz. to 8–10 drops of catalyst. Stir thoroughly.
6. Pour the plastic over the embeddments in the mold up to the top, but do not overflow.
7. Allow the plastic in the mold to dry thoroughly.
8. When dry, and hardened, remove from the mold. If the plastic is difficult to remove, place in a deep freeze for a short period of time.
9. When the plastic is removed from the mold, affix the jewelry finding (pin back, tie clasp back, cuff link back, earring back) to the back of the plastic with glue. Often these findings may be inserted into the top layer of plastic just before it has hardened; then it will set.

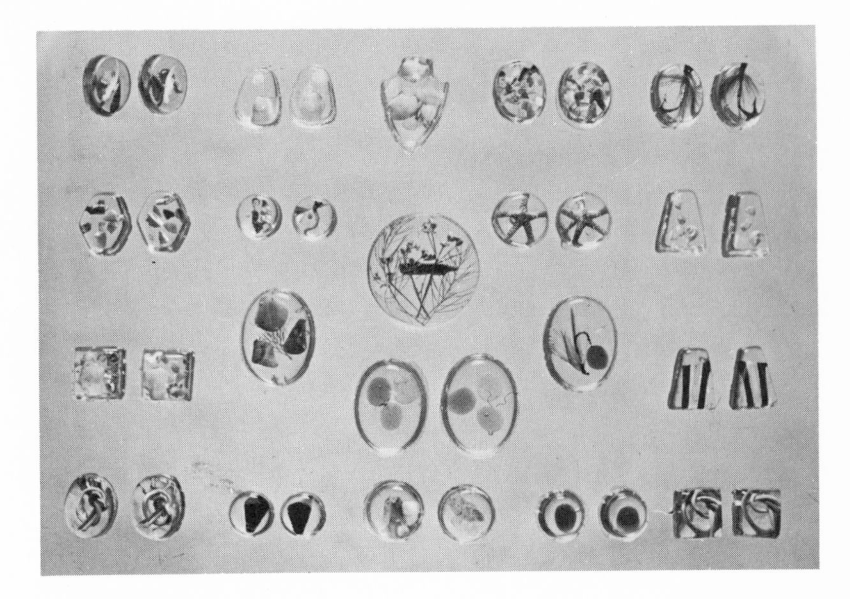

Figure 4. Jewelry

PROJECT 4: DESK SET – PEN HOLDER, PAPER WEIGHT, LETTER OPENER

(Figure 5)

1. Molds for these articles may be purchased from craft stores or made as follows:
   a. Lay heavy duty wax paper on the table.
   b. Form oil base clay around to identify shapes. *(Figure 6)*
2. Treat the mold thoroughly with mold release if it is a commercial mold.
3. Mix the plastic with the catalyst, 1 oz. plastic to 8–10 drops of catalyst.
4. Stir the mixture thoroughly.
5. Pour a layer into each mold (1 oz. is recommended for the first layer of a paper weight or pen set).
6. Allow the first layer to set and become jelly-like.
7. Place the embeddments in the desired position (upside down positionfor those that need be reversed).
8. Mix another formula of plastic and catalyst, 2 oz. plastic and 16–20 drops of catalyst.
9. Stir thoroughly.
10. Pour the plastic mixture in the mold to cover the embeddments; fill to the brim but do not run over.
11. Allow the contents of the mold to set and harden thoroughly.
12. When completely hardened remove from the mold.

NOTE: If you desire to use color in the plastic, it may be done in the following manner:

a. Pour one layer of clear plastic, as directed above.
b. Allow the first layer to set.
c. Mix another formula of plastic and add one *tiny* bit of color. Use a toothpick. Be careful not to use too much color; a little goes a long way.
d. Add the same amount of surface hardener as you did catalyst.
e. Stir thoroughly.
f. Pour the mixture into the mold, over the embeddments.
g. When both layers are hard remove from the mold.

Figure 5. Desk set (pen holder, paper weight, letter opener)

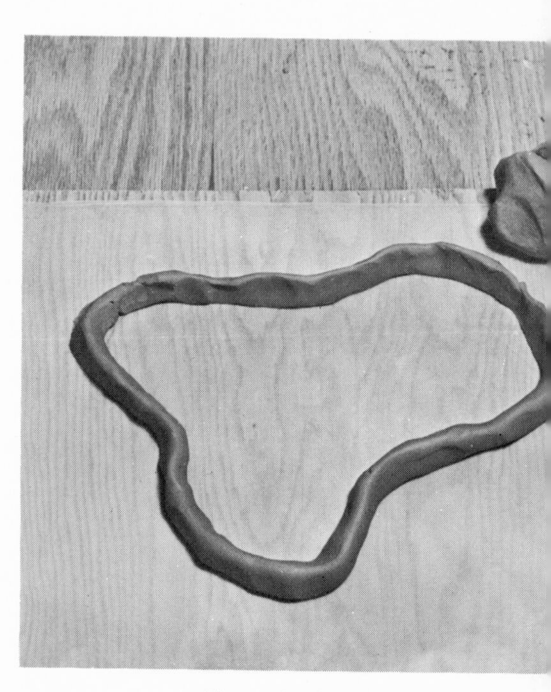

Figure 6. Oil base clay form

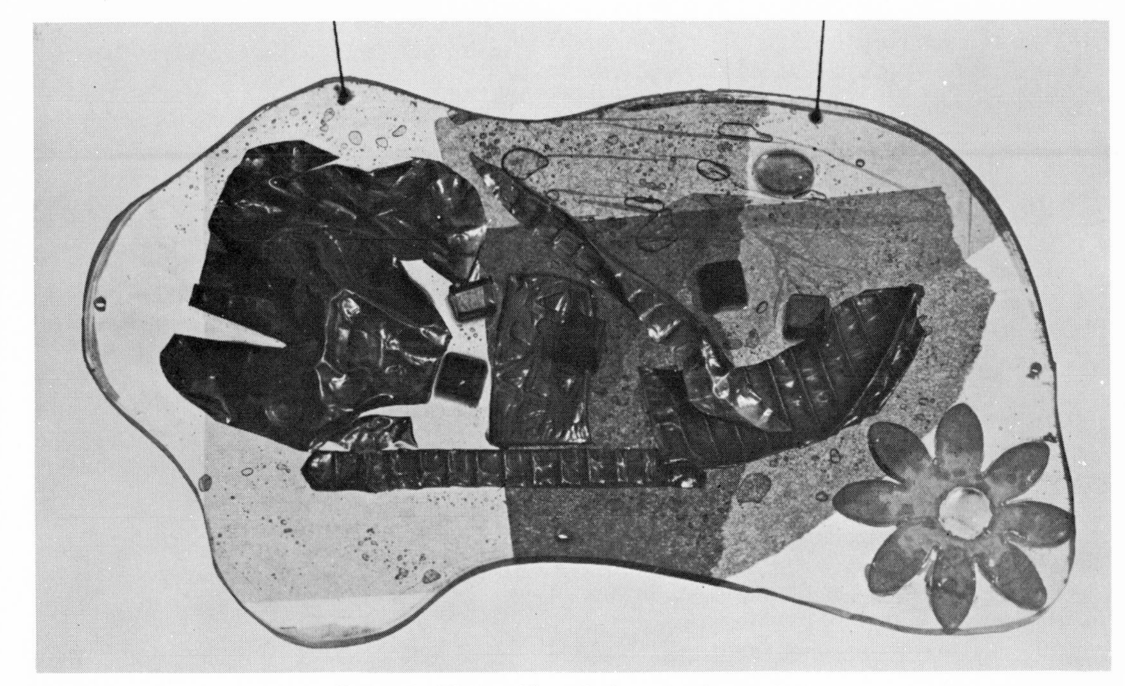

Figure 7. Wall and/or window plastic hanging

Figure 8. Wall and/or window plastic hanging

PROJECT 5: WALL AND/OR WINDOW PLASTIC HANGING *(Figure 7)*

1. Form a shape on heavy duty waxpaper, using oil base clay as the dam to outline (Note *Figure 6).*
2. Set the embeddments. The example shows colored tissue paper, metal tooling, and square plastic forms.
3. Mix the plastic, 1 oz. plastic to 8–10 drops of catalyst. A piece of 8" x 10" size requires about 4 ozs. of plastic. A piece 18" x 4' as in *Figure 8*,, requires 44 ozs. of plastic and 440 drops of catalyst. (This is 8–10 drops of catalyst to 1 oz. plastic.)
4. If color is desired, note Project 4, step 12, and follow the step-by-step process, pouring one layer at a time.
5. When the plastic is hard, remove the oil base clay dam and peal off the waxpaper. If the edges are rough, they may be sawed, filed, or ground off.

PROJECT 6: PLASTIC TABLE *(Figure 9)*

1. The example in the figure was made on top of a round piece of glass, 18" in diameter and approximately ¼" thick. The glass is placed on a level, solid surface. You will need two quarts of casting resin for this project.
2. Form a dam around the glass. Oil base clay with modeling metal is good, as in *Figure 9.*
3. Pour a layer of plastic about ¼" thick on top of the glass. This will take 20 ozs. of plastic and 200 drops of catalyst. (This is equivalent to 3½ teaspoons.) Be sure you stir these together thoroughly before pouring.
4. Allow this layer to stand undisturbed until gelled. (Approximately 30 minutes.)
5. Place the embeddments onto the layer of plastic, remembering to reverse them so the desired side will be on top when out of the mold.
6. Mix another formula of plastic, about 20 ozs. of plastic and 175 drops of catalyst (approximately 3 teaspoons.)
7. If color is desired, add a very small amount. Use a toothpick. A little color goes a long way. If color is added also add surface hardener. The amount of surface hardener should be equal to the amount of catalyst.
8. Pour the mixture of plastic over the embeddments and allow to set and harden (at least 1 hour).
9. A third layer of clear plastic may now be added, if desired. To do this, mix 20 ozs. of plastic and 200 drops of catalyst (approximately 3½ teaspoons). Pour clear plastic over the colored plastic which is now thoroughly set.
10. When the final layer of plastic is hardened, which will take several hours, remove the dam.
11. Smooth rough edges with sandpaper. The opaque white quality caused by sandpaper may be made transparent by mixing 1 oz. casting resin and 10 drops of catalyst and touching up with a brush.
12. Your plastic tabletop is now ready for fastening legs of your choice. *Figures 10* and *11* show other examples which may be explored.

Figure 9. Plastic table top

Figure 10. Trivet

Figure 11. Paper weight

WEAVING

Tools & Materials needed:

Basics

- loom (loop, spool, or flat loom)
- shuttles (flat)
- bridges
- needles
- crochet hooks (various sizes)
- yarn

Represented below are four examples of simple looms which could easily be made at home from scrap lumber such as that found in old shipping crates. *(Figure 1)* A very soft white pine has the best properties for loom construction.

Loom A *(Figure 1)* is a loop loom, easily constructed from an 8" square board set with rows of nails. The nails are ½" high, ½" apart, and ½" from each edge, forming a 7" square of nails. All the nails used in making these looms should be 1¼" wire finishing nails (15 gauge). Note that the corners are left without nails, because they are unnecessary. A simple hammer can be used for driving the nails, but it is recommended that the holes be punched with an awl or drilled most of the depth with a 1/16" bit.

Looms B and C *(Figure 1)* are spool type looms. Loom B is made from an empty thread spool with about a 5/16" hole. By spacing five nails equally around the hole about ¼" from it, an excellent little loom can be constructed for weav-

Figure 1. Looms

ing small coils. For the weaving of heavy coils such as rug might require, simply construct a larger type of spool loom – loom C *(Figure 1)*. Such a loom can be made by drilling a 1" hole in the center of a 3/4" thick block of wood and nailing it on two small legs 2" high. Nails should be placed in the same manner as that mentioned for the small spool. The diameter of the hole will vary depending upon the thickness of the yarn used since the coil being formed should fit loosely through the opening.

Loom D *(Figure 1)* is a slot loom and is formed by placing two boards, 20" long, 1¼" wide, and ¾" deep, parallel to each other about ½" apart. Next, nail a 3" square block to each end to act as legs. The slot formed between the long boards gives the loom its name. Start the rows of nails in 1" from each end. They should be ½" high, ¼" apart, and ¼" from the slot. This loom can be almost any length depending on the width of the project involved.

Loom E *(Figure 1)* is a flat loom and is constructed of two end pieces, 2½" high, 1½" wide, and 14" long, plus two side pieces, 1 5/8" high, 1" wide, and 21" long. Slots are cut across the end pieces ¼" apart and ¼" deep down the length of the boards. The two end pieces are connected by nailing the two side boards to their base. Instead of slots, nails could be used as in the other looms. There are two drawbacks to this: (1) the nails placed ¼" apart may spit the wood, and (2) the weft would have to start and end a couple of inches in from the nails as to leave enough warp to tie up the ends. *(Figure 18)*

All the measurements of the boards forming the above looms are dependent upon what scrap is available and can be altered in size according to the project.

Shuttles and bridges (See F in *Figure 1*) can be made from stiff cardboard or a thin piece of wood. The shuttles have notches in the ends and serve as a storage for the weft threads and as a guide to aid in picking through the warp threads. The bridges are unnotched and form a shed for the return trip of the shuttle. *(Figure 13)*

The needles shown in G of *Figure 1* are also used to pick and guide the weft through the warp, especially when the shuttles can no longer be used for this purpose.

Item H of *Figure 1* pictures a group of commercial crochet hooks which range in size from a number five to a large unnumbered hook. They are of use in the looping of threads for certain kinds of weaving.

Figure 2. Yarns

Figure 2 shows the various yarns which are commercially available.

It is an educated guess that weaving, man's oldest craft, is about ten thousand years old. A web of materials woven together to catch fish might have been a logical beginning for weaving with such utilitarian items as mats and baskets coming soon thereafter. Making cloth would have been a bit more complicated since it depends on finding the proper fibers and rendering them into strands. The basics of weaving remain unchanged, however, for the fundamental weaves were established before the time of Christ.

Because the basic methods and weaves lend themselves to endless variety and creativity, the art of weaving is a basic one and lends itself well to use in schools. As well as developing manual dexterity in its simplest form, weaving also stresses good taste and aesthetic judgement in color, texture, and design. This art combines the creative and the useful and is now fostered by many schools and is an integral part of their programs. Although some weavers are professionally employed by designers, decorators, and textile industries, most enjoy their craft as a pleasurable avocation.

The craft of weaving is a delightful and creative combination of texture, design, and color. The rewards of even the simplest project lie in its utility and attractiveness. Beginning weavers should use the most basic weaving materials and move gradually with their new knowledge and skill to the more complex looms and weaving apparatus. Some will always be content with the endless combinations of the loop loom, and others will prefer the projects on the slot loom.

Weaving is suited to the simplest needs of the very young and very old, and at the same time is challenging and ever-varied for even the most vigorous man or woman. This age-old craft takes many forms and has much to offer all who take it up. It is an adventure—and a most exciting one.

The following projects will serve as an adequate, basic introduction to weaving. They have been especially designed to demonstrate that elaborate equipment is unnecessary. Emphasis has been placed on the simplicity and usefulness of the project and the ready availability of the weaving device due to simple construction and low cost.

PROJECT 1: POT HOLDER (Loop Loom)

(Figure 3)

1. Purchase a bag of loops from a dimestore, hobby shop, or variety store. *(Figure 4)*
2. Take the loop loom and stretch the loops between opposite nails going in one direction. These are the warp threads through which the weft threads will be woven. Alternate these warp threads in groups of colors to form a plaid pattern.
3. Take a loop, and, starting on the first nail going in the opposite direction, weave the loop under and over each loop of the warp until you reach the opposite nail. This is the beginning of the weft. Starting on the next nail weave another loop over-under-over-under the opposite of the first weft loop. Continue weaving loops in this alternating fashion *(Figure 5)* until all the nails are filled. This is the most basic and common weave known, the plain weave or tabby weave.
4. Using a large crochet hook (00 or larger) and starting at any corner loop, slip it and its neighboring loop off of their nails and draw the second loop *(Figure 6)* through the first. Now pick up the third loop and continue until you have drawn the last loop through. Stretching this last loop and knotting it thru itself will prevent it from unweaving, and it will act as a holding loop for hanging purposes.

   NOTE: To prevent the pot holder from slipping off of its nails while looping the edge together, hook the corner loops to the nails after they have been interwoven. *(Figure 6)*

Figure 3. Pot holder

Figure 4. Loops

Figure 5. Stretched loops

Figure 6. Remove from frame

PROJECT 2: HOT PAD (Spool Loom)
(Figure 7)

1. This project calls for a spool type loom with a 1" diameter. (Loom C, *Figure 1*) Select about 70 yards of a heavy four-ply cotton or wool rug yarn to make this hot pad. (A cotton or a cotton combination such as 50% rayon and 50% cotton would probably be best because these are washable.) Wool would be best if you are contemplating making a rug on this loom. If your yarn comes in a skein form, it would be advisable to roll it into a ball before starting.
2. Start by passing the end of the thread down through the hole. Then loop the yarn clockwise around every second nail until each nail has been warped and a star pattern is formed. *(Figure 8)*
3. Now start a second loop around the first nail forming a second row of yarn. Taking a large crochet hook, like the one used in Project 1, lift the lower loop out and up over the top of the nail, leaving only the new loop of yarn remaining. Continue around the spool skipping to every second nail, forming a new loop, and lifting the bottom loop over the top one.
4. The continuation of this process will form a coil growing down through the hole in the spool. If a change of color is desired, tie the end of the yarn together and push the knot into the center of the coil.
5. Secure and hide the end thread by weaving it back into the center of the coil *(Figure 9)* or by sewing it down inconspicuously to the side of the coil.
6. The sewing of the hot pad can begin as soon as the coil has reached 15" to 20" long. It is desirable to start at this time to prevent the excess coil from becoming knotted or tangled. Using some of the same yarn, or a strong thread of a matching color, sew or lace the coils together around and around in a circular fashion. A curved needle *(Figure 26)* would be helpful for this type of sewing, but a straight one can serve just as well.
7. Alternating between weaving the coil and sewing it together continue until you have created a hot pad about 8" in diameter. When you wish to stop, cut the thread and draw the end through all five loops *(Figure 10)*, securing the end thread as described in step 5 and shown in *Figure 9*. Sew up the remaining coil, and your hot pad is finished.

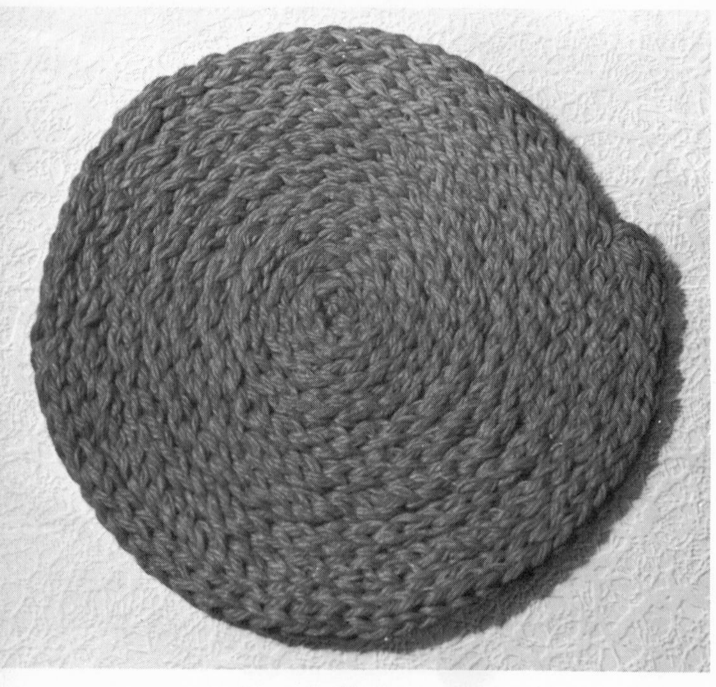

Figure 7. Hot pad

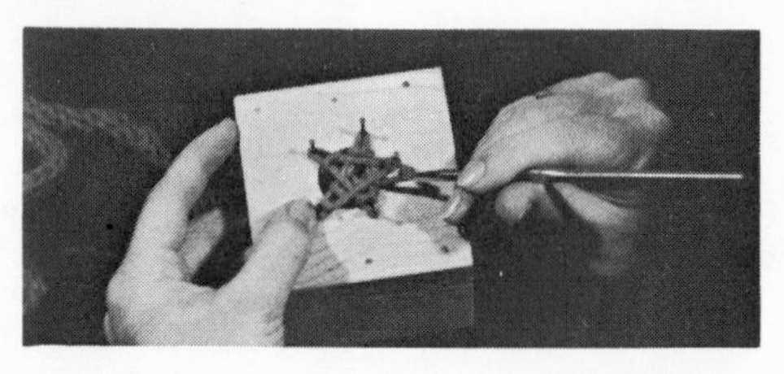

Figure 8. Put end of thread through hole

Figure 9. Hide end of thread

Figure 10. Finish

PROJECT 3: PLACE MAT (Flat Loom)
(Figure 11)

1. There are many types of yarn that could be used for this project. For an everyday place mat choose cotton or a cotton combination so that the mat can be easily washed. For a dressier mat, wool might be used. Often a large number of coarse materials like straw, raffia, match sticks, twine, and bamboo are used in place mats to develop variety and texture.
2. For this project take one or two ply, or larger, wool thread. Knot it either behind the first slot or loop it around the first slot of the flat loom. (Loom E, *Figure 1*) Then take the thread across the loom and through the first opposite slot and lead it around the back through the second slot. Continue this process of warping the loom one slot at a time, *(Figure 12)* warping the entire loom. Do not pull the warp tight, but leave a little slack for the weft thread to take up.
3. Now take a bridge (F, *Figure 1*), slightly longer than the width of the warp. Interweave the warp in the tabby fashion–under, over, under, over, etc.–across the warp. When this bridge is turned perpendicular to the warp threads, it will raise the odd threads and lower the even threads, or vice versa. *(Figure 13)*
4. Wind the same thread that composed the warp on a shuttle for use as part of the weft. Starting at the right and using the end of the shuttle as a guide *(Figure 14)*, nose it over, under, over in an opposite fashion to that of the bridge. Leave a 2" or 3" over-hang on the beginning thread to tuck in to the next shed so it will be locked, *(Figure 13)* and hidden in the weaving itself.
5. Now turn the bridge perpendicular to form the shed *(Figure 13)*, and slide the shuttle back across the warp to form the second thread of the weft. Tuck the beginning thread in now, and pack the second thread up tight against the first by turning the bridge horizontal again and using it to push the threads straight and together. *(Figure 15)*
6. Continue weaving in this fashion until you are ready to change color or type of thread. Finish and start all new threads by the overhanging method mentioned in steps 4 and 5. *(Figure 13)*
7. To make weaving of the weft simpler, it is desirable to weave from both ends of the loom so as to avoid pulling the warp threads out of their slots. *(Figure 14)* When the warp becomes so closed with weft that the bridge won't turn and the shuttle doesn't have room you will have to finish the tabby weave with a wooden needle (G, *Figure 1 and Figure 16*) and finally by hand. *(Figure 17)*
8. After completing the weft, all that remains is to cut the warp threads at the end *(Figure 18)* and tie them up, two or three in a bunch. Make certain that the knot is pulled tight against the weft so that it will not unravel. *(Figure 19)* These bunches can then be braided in a decorative effect to lie as a frill on the ends. They can also be sewn under the mat so they will not show.

Figure 11. Flat loom place mat

Figure 12. Warp loom

Figure 13. Bridge

Figure 14. Use shuttle to pass yarn under bridge

Figure 15. Push threads together

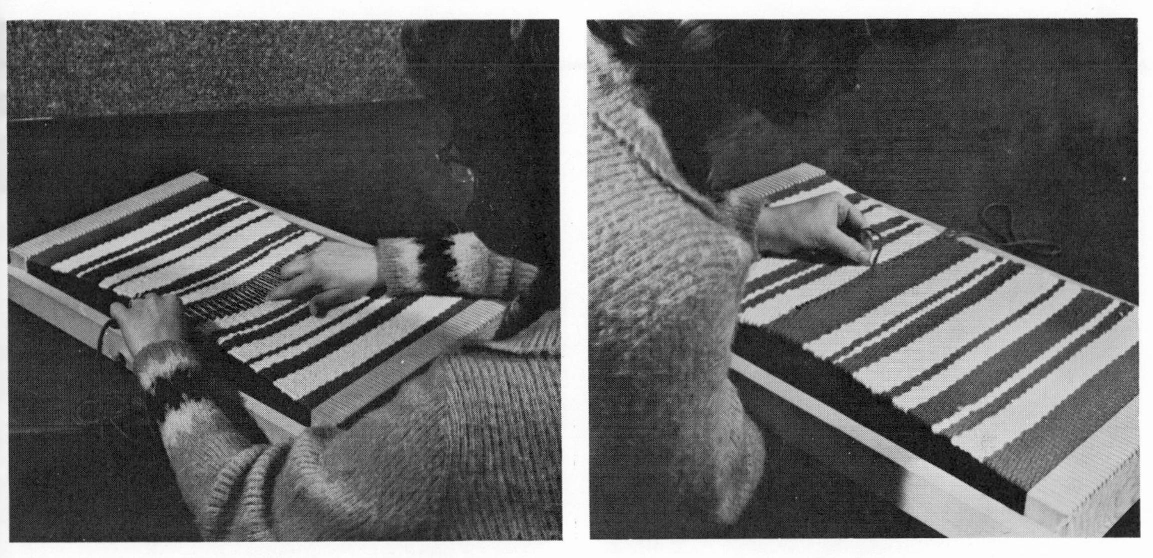

Figure 16. Continue with wooden needle

Figure 17. Finish by hand

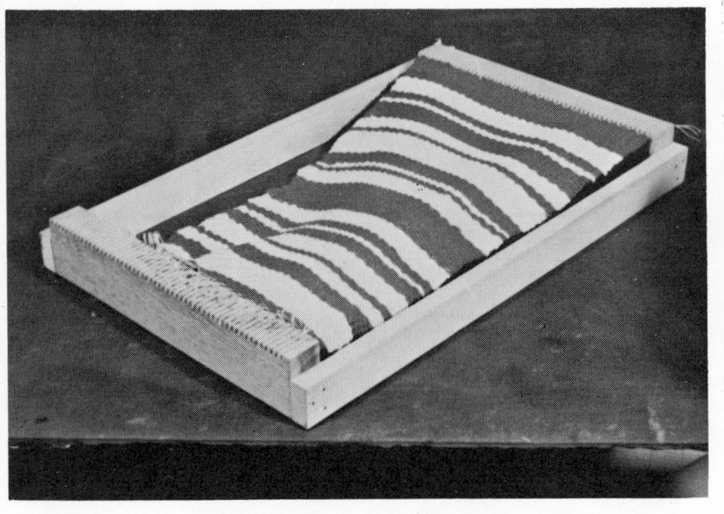

Figure 18. Cut warp threads

Figure 19. Both ends of warp threads are cut

PROJECT 4: SCARF (Slot Loom)

(Figure 20)

1. The slot loom (D, *Figure 1*) produces a flat length of woven material and is best for making heavily textured projects. Choose a heavy three or four ply cotton or wool yarn for this project.
2. Tie a small loop in the beginning thread and slip it over the first nail. Then loop the thread around the first nail on the opposite side of the slot. Return it and loop it around the second nail on the first side. Continue in this fashion down the loom for as great a distance as is desired for the width of the scarf. In this case a 12" width is used. *(Figure 21)*
3. Turn around the end nail and start back *(Figure 21)*, looping another layer of threads around the same nails. This will create a second layer directly on top of the first. It will be loose until the bottom layer of loops is brought up and over the top of the nails as described in step 3 of Project 2. Do this going down one side of the loom at a time. *(Figure 22)*
4. Continue this process. The end nail in each layer is used for turning and will be woven off only on alternating layers. Keep the loops rather loose on the nails so that you can weave faster and more uniformly. The scarf will form down through the slot in the loom *(Figure 22)* and should be pulled slightly after the looping of each layer. This will prevent the scarf from piling up in the slot.

Figure 20. Slot loom scarf

5. Scarfs are usually 30" to 36" long. When weaving has reached the desired length, cut off the yarn, leaving an 18" length. Pull this end through each loop, alternating back and forth from side to side as you did when weaving the scarf. *(Figure 23)* After pulling the end of the yarn through the last loop, interweave it back into the scarf *(Figure 9)* or sew it down inconspicuously.

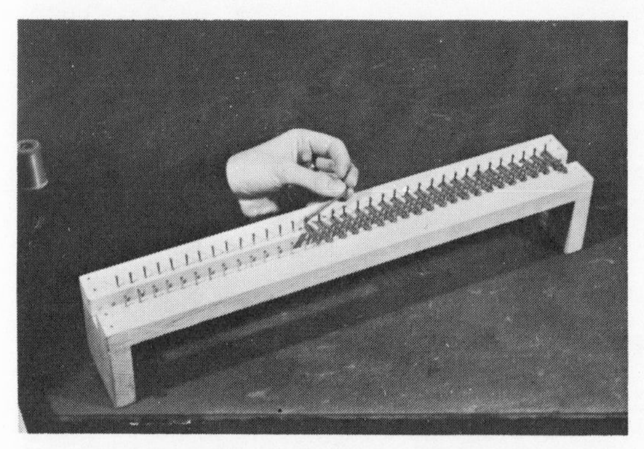

Figure 21. Threading slot loom

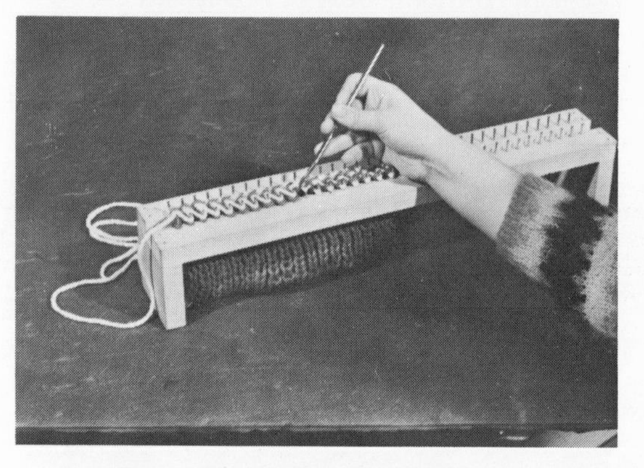

Figure 22. Weaving on slot loom

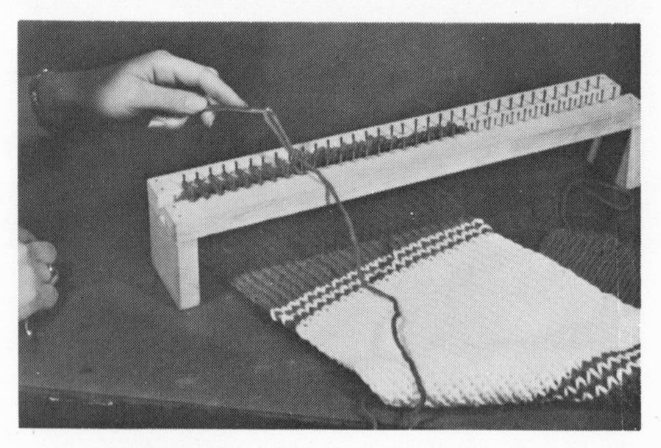

Figure 23. Scarf from slot loom

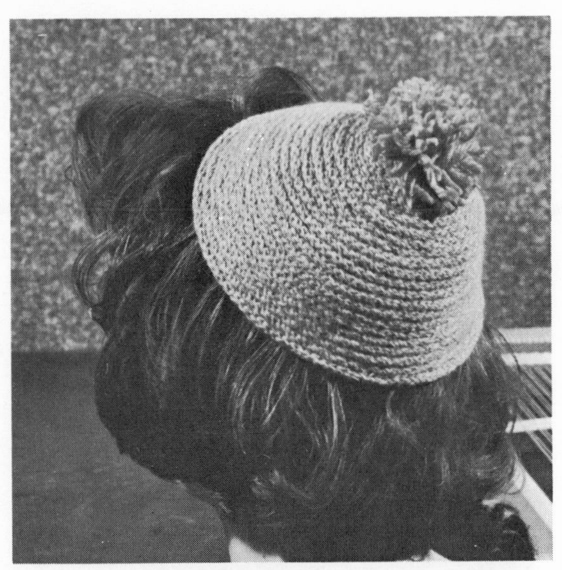
Figure 24. Spool type hat

PROJECT 5: HAT (Spool Type)
(Figure 24)

1. For this project use the large thread spool (B, *Figure 1*) and fairly heavy crochet cotton or single ply wool yarn. Follow steps 2 thru 7 of Project 2, the hot pad.
2. The only change in this procedure will occur when you are ready to start sewing the coil together to form the hat. Instead of laying the coil out flat on the table, you should form it over an appropriately sized and shaped bowl. *(Figure 25)* Sew or lace the coils together at the angle of the curve being used. *(Figure 26)*
3. To finish this project, you can buy a pom-pom or make one. *(Figure 24)* To make the pom-pom warp a bunch of yarn around a 3" piece of cardboard, slide it off tying it in the middle, cut the loops at each end, and fluff it. (See steps in *Figure 27.*)

Figure 25. Form coil over bowl shape

Figure 27. Pom-Pom

Figure 26. Sew on lace coils together

PROJECT 6: PILLOW CASE (Flat Loom)
(Figure 28)

Figure 28. Flat loom pillow case

1. The project is quite similar to Project 3, the place mat. Again the flat loom is used. (E, *Figure 1*) Those directions indicated in steps 1 thru 8 of Project 3 should be followed. The only difference is in the use of heavy cotton rug yarn of 2 contrasting colors for this project. With this create a design of irregular width stripes. *(Figure 18)*
2. To complete this project *(Figure 28)*, fold the finished piece of material in half, bottom side out, and sew up two sides by hand or machine. *(Figure 29)*
3. Turn the case right side out and stuff the pillow with old love letters, feathers, kapok, foam, or almost anything. Used in *Figure 30* are bits of foam rubber which are sold commercially for this purpose.
4. Sew up the third side.

Figure 29. Sew up sides

Figure 30. Stuff pillow case

Tools and Materials needed:

Basics
- wood
- knife (pocket knife or carver's knife)
- razor blade (single edge)
- paint (oil, water colors)
- graphite paper
- shellac
- sandpaper

Extras
- chisels (flat blades; V shaped, called a veiner)
- gouges (curved blades)
- mallet (round, hardwood)
- ruler
- pencil
- compass
- whetstone
- bench
- clamps (C clamps)
- steel wool
- varnish
- linseed oil
- turpentine
- pumice-stone or rotten-stone
- wax
- glue

WOOD

Wood is a friendly, natural material. Woodworking is a fine basic craft. From the great trees that grow from a seed in the earth we build homes and shelters against the elements. Man has never been satisfied, however, with mere shells to keep out the winter winds. He has taken these basic essentials and enhanced them. Wood, consequently, has become decorative and aesthetic, as well as practical. To know and understand the many kinds of wood is a study in itself.

Probably no one knows when man first discovered he could shape wood. Perhaps it was when he needed a spear or a tool handle for practical use in his survival. As it became easier for him to make needed utensils, he soon had the desire to see the utensil not only practical but also decorative.

Today, woodcarving is important in many countries. Switzerland carries on carving as a major occupation. Sweden has done much in carving, as have all Scandinavian countries. Most of the carving and decorating of wood in America was introduced by early settlers from Northern Europe.

Wood is one of the most inexpensive crafts. You may begin with a simple box or a block of wood and one tool. Many kinds of wood are suitable and beautiful for carving and decorating. The

Figure 1. Mexican carving

type most satisfactory for beginners in carving is Idaho White Pine because it is straight grained and soft. California Redwood planking and walnut are good, as are sugar pine, white pine, basswood, cottonwood, and sumac. In general, soft woods with less pronounced grains will give best results for the beginner. If hard woods are used, gum, mahogany, maple, and black walnut are good.

For wood finishes, smooth the work with fine sandpaper, pumice-stone, or rotten-stone. The latter should be used on a soft rag or a paint brush. These will not scratch the wood so you may work it in all directions.

Generally speaking, avoid the use of stains. Use varnish (sparingly), white shellac (two coats – good for soft woods), and linseed oil (best for dark woods). Use eight or more coats (the first should be one-half linseed oil and one-half turpentine applied hot, and beeswax heated and applied.)

In selecting woods remember the following:

a. Choose straight grained woods for carving.
b. Avoid knots or burl grain in wood for carving.
c. Ornamental grain does not require further decoration.

Our purpose is to introduce to you several different practical, as well as aesthetic, projects where wood is the medium of expression.

PROJECT 1: CHIP CARVED BOX
(Figure 2)

1. Select a wooden box made of soft wood.
2. The design is made primarily of simple triangles bisected. Continue the bisecting lines until they meet at the center of the figures. The most complicated looking designs are made of nothing but common triangles. If you can carve just one triangle, you can easily carve a whole design. Form your triangles together to complete the design in all-over, border, or "frame" repeats. Draw your design on paper the size of your box, then trace it with graphite paper on the box.
3. Take an old piece of soft wood which is smooth and straight grained. Practice on this. Draw some triangles and bisect their angles to form designs. Draw several shapes. Use a single-edged razor blade as in *Figure 3*, a knife, or a chisel. If you use a chisel, the sharp end of the skew is called the point and the other end of the cutting edge is called the heel. *(Figure 4)*

   Place the point of the chisel at the point where all bisectors meet and keep the chisel perpendicular to the wood. Now, with the wooden mallet, pound the point of the chisel down into the wood. The cut must be right along the bisectors of the angles of the triangle. When the cut reaches the vertex of the angle, cease pounding. Repeat this process on the other two bisectors of the triangle. Now all three bisector lines are cut. These cuts are referred to as the stab. *(Figure 5)*
4. After practice, proceed directly to your good box and carve slowly and carefully.
5. Finish as suggested in the introduction.

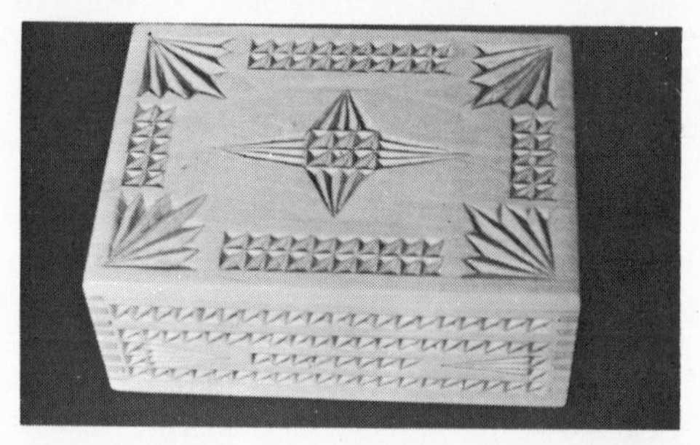

Figure 2. Chip carving

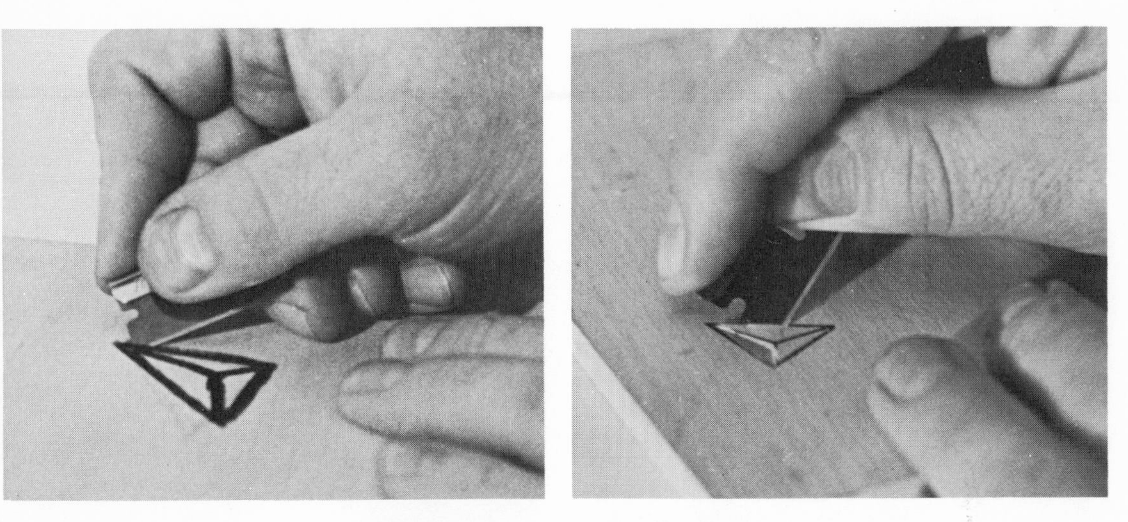

Figure 3. Cut with single edge razor

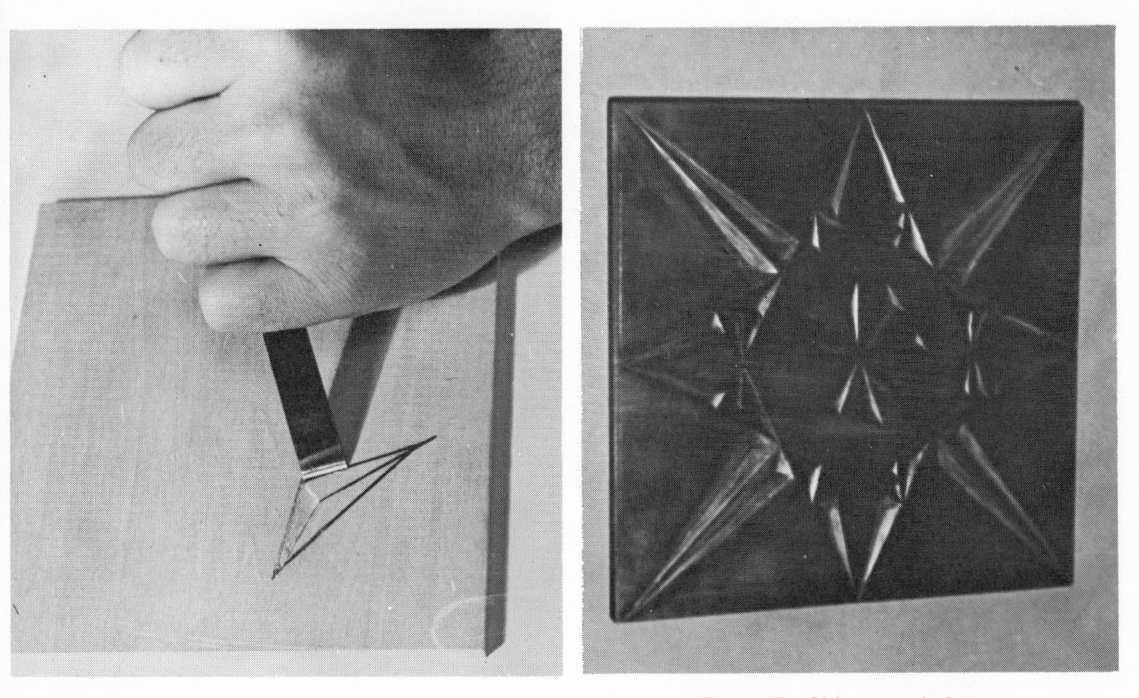

Figure 4. Using a chisel

Figure 5. Chip carved plaque

PROJECT 2: RELIEF CARVING AND PAINTING *(Figure 6)*

1. Select a soft wood (white pine) "turned" plate. Pressed plates are not good because they are usually made of hard wood and often warp easily. Sand and smooth the plate.
2. Plan a design on paper which fits the size and movement of the round shape of the plate as shown in *Figure 6.* Designs to fit the rim, the center, or even both are fine. Plan your colors. Trace the design onto the wooden plate with graphite paper.
3. Along some lines (not necessarily all) cut directly and straight down into the wood. Use a single-edged razor blade or a sharp knife such as an x-acto knife. Next, about ¼" away from the cut make another cut at an angle toward the original straight cut. This will peel out a strip of wood and form your design into a "relief" effect. Cut away whenever you want to emphasize lines. This may be the entire design. After all carving is complete, smooth with sandpaper and pumice.
4. Oil or water paints may be used. If a transparent color is desired (showing the grain of the wood through it), use transparent water colors. If an opaque effect is desired, use either tempera or oil paints. Use any paint which is quite dry. A watery paint will run into the pores. Often one coat of filler is put into the wood to help prevent the running. When using oil paint, thin to a usable consistency with linseed oil and turpentine.
5. Because the carved piece was sanded smooth before painting, this finish applies only to the final protective coat which may be white shellac or wax. If shellac is used, apply one coat after the paint is thoroughly dry. Allow this to dry thoroughly also. Rub with steel wool. Apply another coat. After this coat is dry, rub it down a little with steel wool if a dull finish is desired.

   If wax is used, simply apply the wax to the plate after the paint is thoroughly dry. Use a soft cloth. Rub to the desired finish.

   There are now good commercial varnish and plastic sprays available. Ask for them at craft or hardware stores.

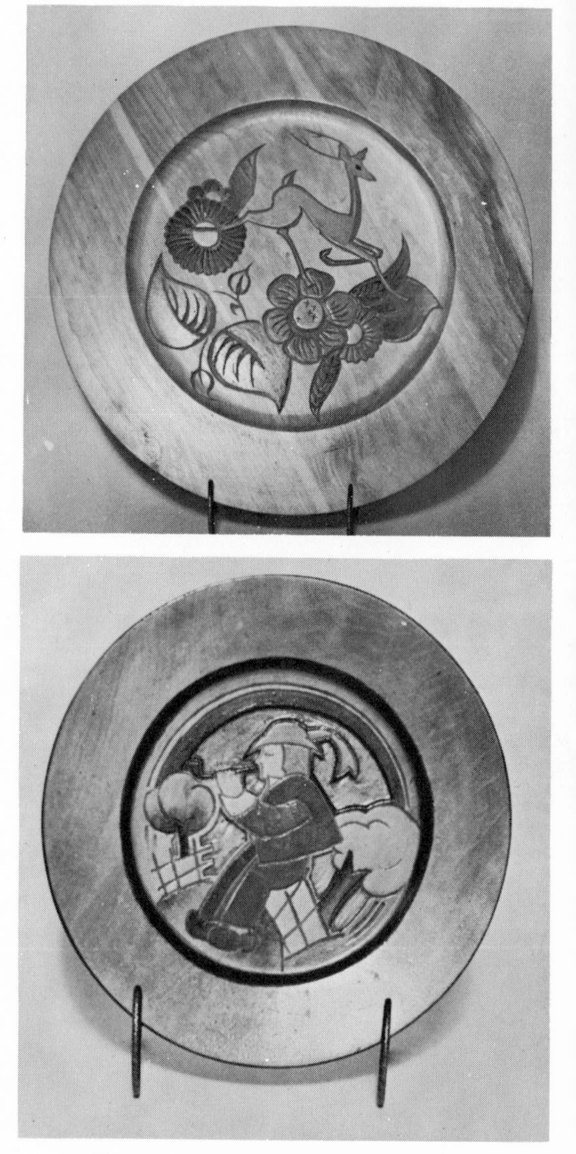

Figure 6. Relief carving and painting

PROJECT 3: PAINTED WOODEN BOWL, FORK AND SPOON *(Figure 7)*

1. The wooden bowl and fork and spoon can be purchased at craft stores (even at hardware stores) in various sizes. They are unfinished. Sand and wipe the bowl and utensils.
2. Because these bowls are generally used to serve tossed salads, paintings of fruits and vegetables are appropriate. *(Figure 7)* This is not a rule, however. Abstract designs of various types are always possible. If you use the fruit and vegetable idea, look in seed and feed catalogues as well as ads for soups or tomato juice. These give good pictures of the subjects to guide you. Draw these subjects, cut them out, and trace them on the clean smooth bowl so that they decorate the top part of the bowl (both inside and out). There is no reason for painting the inside bottom or the outside bottom of the bowl. Apply a similar motif to the handles of the fork and spoon.
3. These bowls are usually made from hard wood and do not have an especially nice grain. Therefore, oil paint is suggested for the color. Thin your tube oil paint slightly with linseed oil and turpentine. Paint flat or bring out high-lights and shadows if you wish.
4. When the color is dry and well set, the bowl and utensils should have a good hard finish to withstand hot water and hard detergents. Wiping or soft washing after each use is sufficient. A hard, flint top varnish which is neat and water resistand should be used. It may be purchased at hardware stores and should be applied as directed. (Clear bar top varnish is good.)

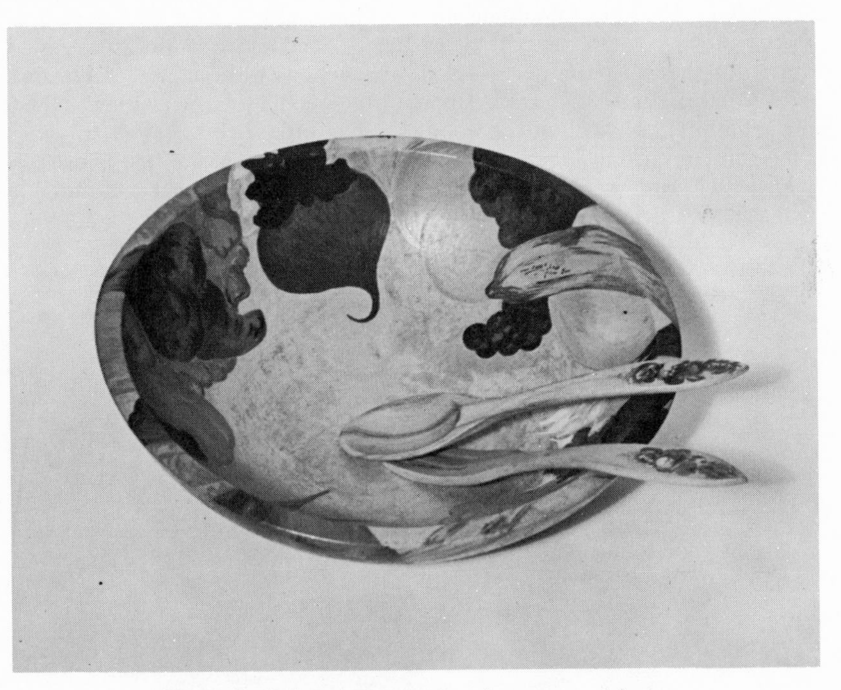

Figure 7. Painted wooden bowl, spoon and fork

PROJECT 4: FIGURES AND ABSTRACTIONS *(Figures 8, 9 and 10)*

1. Wood for whittling and carving should be soft. *Figure 8* shows small animals carved out of small, soft pine blocks. The abstract sculpture form in *Figure 10* is from a 5" x 5" x 12" block of sumac.
2. Designs for the simple little animals pictured can be found in magazines, little children's coloring books, or can be drawn free hand. They should be simple and in profile.

Designs for abstract sculpturing such as illustrated in *Figure 10* cannot be found. They are created. The process consists of acquiring a piece of wood, carefully studying the grain, taking chisels, and laboriously carving. This is a purely creative process, which is generally dictated by the grain of the wood and the emotion which you desire to express. The piece illustrated represents many hours of studying, chiseling, smoothing, and finishing.

A. The little carved figures are made out of small blocks of soft wood about 2" x 3" x 4". Draw your silhouettes in profile model on the wood. Block out this form by cutting directly through the block *(Figure 11)* with a coping saw or jigsaw. Form the animals as follows:
   1. Round square corners to form a round body, head, and legs.
   2. Divide the ears so there is a left and a right.
   3. Carve the space between the legs to form a right and left.
   4. Carve off parts of the tail and nose so they become growths of the middle of the back and the head.

B. To form a man such as the blocked form of *Figure 11,* proceed as follows:
   1. Round all parts. (This gives a brim to the hat all around.)
   2. Carve the front and back to form arms in the middle of the body; part, left and right.
   3. Divide the legs to make a right and a left.
   4. Soften, sand, and add details as desired.

C. To form a piece of abstract sculpture such as *Figure 10,* study the wood, place the block of sumac (about 5" x 5" x 12") or other wood into a vice. Clamp tightly.

With chisels and mallet start cutting away parts. Turn, cut, turn, cut, study, turn, and cut. Make some parts deeper and some longer in their cuts.

Sand and smooth (as suggested in the introduction) with pumice. All figures and sculpturing should then be inviting to the touch. Shellac the little figures (at least two coats, rubbed down between the first and second coat). Wax and rub the abstract sculptured piece to obtain the desired finish and shine.

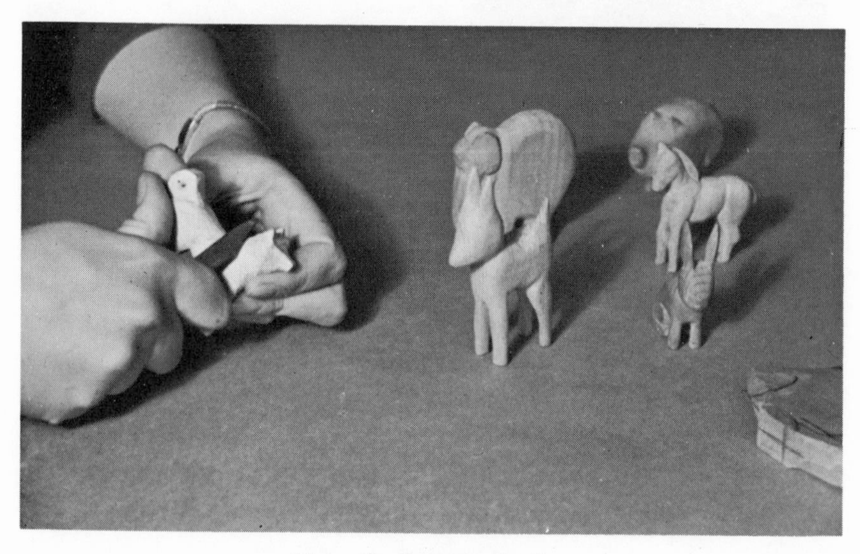

Figure 8. Carved animals

Figure 9. Carved figures

Figure 10. Carved abstract form

Figure 11. Block cut figure

Figure 12. Wood cut mural

PROJECT 5: WOOD CUT AND WALL MURAL *(Figure 12)*

The wood cut was discussed in the chapter on *Application of Design to Fabrics,* but, because this project involves a wood process, projects are also suggested here.

1. Wood for the wood cut should be soft. The size depends upon the desired use of the finished print. Prints from wood cuts are used for Christmas cards, book plates, wall decorations, and a host of other purposes. A certain exciting effect is achieved by making large cuts such as our example here. It is 18" x 24".
2. Plan a black and white design the size of the wood. Plan so the blacks will be cut out and the whites left standing (or vice versa). Often times, we paint the block black and draw on our design. Then, as we cut away, we begin to see the black and white contrast. *(Figure 13)* Black and white areas should be interestingly spaced, located, and balanced.
3. A sample of the cutting is shown in *Figure 14. Keep your idle hand away from the cutting tool,* since a slip in cutting is very possible and the gouges are sharp. Generally speaking, you should cut with the grain.
4. The printing is done as described in the chapter on *Application of Design to Fabrics.* However, most wood cuts for a mural or wall decoration are printed on paper. A paper called "silk span" tableau, or rice paper is especially suited to these prints. *Figure 15* shows a pine wood panel cut with small pieces of colored mosaic glued in to make an abstract wall plaque.

Figure 13. Cutting the wood shows black and white areas

Figure 14. Cut the wood with cutting tool

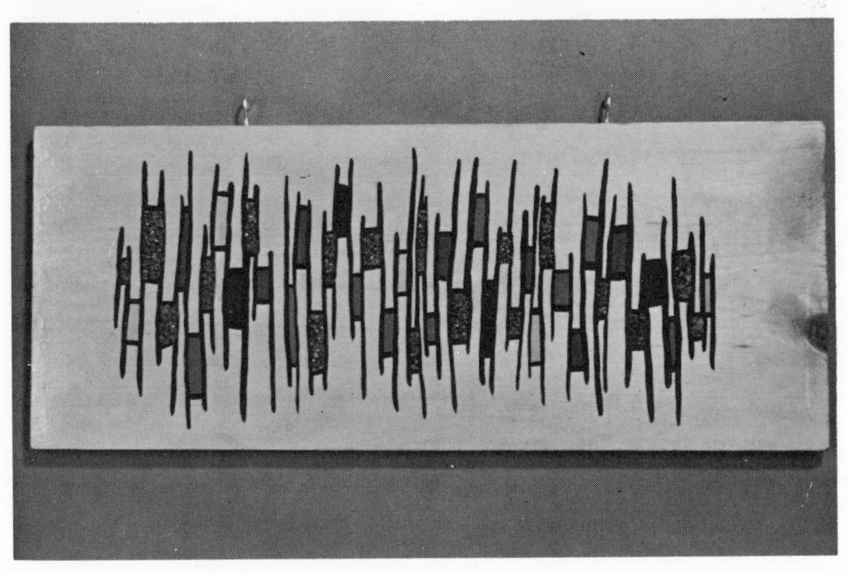

Figure 15. Cut wood panel with mosaic color inlay

PROJECT 6: BOOK REST *(Figure 16)*

Materials for this project are as follows:

Poplar, cypress, chestnut, oak, mahogany, or other woods – rough sizes. One piece for the bottom, ¾" x 6¼" x 4¼"; one upright piece, ¾" x 6¼" x 6¾"; one piece for the tilting support, ¾" x 1¾" x 6¾"; sand paper, glue, and finishes.

Tools:

Pencil, ruler, tri-square, knife, plane, chisels, mallet, clamp or handscrew, sand paper block.

Study the photo carefully. For the roughing operations, add ¼" to the dimensions of the plan. After the three pieces are cut into their sizes, proceed by squaring the pieces to the size indicated in the plans. Use a plane and a tri-square.

Lay out with a pencil the housed dado joint and common dado joint as shown in the plans. Groove the bottom wood piece to allow for insertion of the dado joints. The housed dado joint is the one at the left in the picture. The common dado joint is the full groove into which the bottom leg sets at the right. They are ¾" wide. The housed dado joint and the common dado joint are formed with a mallet and a narrow chisel. Be careful not to make your dado joints too large; this will cause a loose fit.

With sand paper and sand paper block, sand all the parts. Assemble the parts and adjust the clamps. Use blocks or strips of wood to protect the surfaces from injury by the clamps. Disassemble, glue, reassemble, square, and reclamp.

After the glue has dried, remove the hardened glue with a chisel and touch up with sand paper where necessary.

The book rest is now ready for its finish.

Figure 16. Book rest

PROJECT 7: ROCKING HORSE *(Figure 17)*

This functional child's toy is made as follows:

A. Prepare the following materials:

- 1 piece 1" x 12" x 10' wood (clear pine preferably)
- 1 piece ½" wood dowel
- 1 piece leather strap (reins)
- 1 piece leather or felt (ears)
- 1 piece leather or felt (ornament)
- 2 – 1¼" domes of silence (furniture skid buttons)
- 4 – 1¾" number 10 flat head wood screws
- 18 – 1½" number 10 flat head wood screws
- Yarn, rope, or hair (tail)
- Glue

B. Assemble as follows:

1. Glue the sides to the head and to the body spacer.
2. Glue the wedges to the legs. Before gluing determine right and left legs to insure wedges being on the inside of the legs.
3. Drill holes through the legs and fasten them to the body with 1¾" number 10 flat head wood screws.
4. Fasten the leg platform to the legs with 1½" number 10 screws.
5. Fasten the leg platform to the rockers with 1½" number 10 screws.
6. Fasten the ends of the rein to the mouth with a tack.
   a. Fasten the domes of silence over the tacked ends of the rein.
   b. Glue the ornament to the head as pictured.
   c. Fasten the ears to the head with a small screw.
   d. Fasten the tail with a screw eye or staple.
   e. Inset a hand grip in ½" hole in the head. Fasten with glue.

Figure 17. Rocking horse

BIBLIOGRAPHY

APPLICATION OF DESIGN TO FABRICS

American Crayon Company. *Decorate Fabrics With Colors.* Sandusky, Ohio: American Crayon Co., 1943.

Andrews, Michael F. *Creative Printmaking.* New York, N. Y.: Prentice-Hall, Inc., 1964.

Ashton, Pearl F. *Everybody Can Paint Fabrics.* New York, N. Y.: Studio Publishing, Inc., Viking Press, Inc., 1952.

Boylston, Elsie R. *Creative Expression With Crayons.* Worchester, Mass.: The Davis Press, Inc., 1954.

Cliffe, Henry. *Litho-Graphy.* New York, N. Y.: Watson–Guptill Publishing, 1965.

Connors, Dorothy. *Gadgets Galore.* Chicago, Ill.: Popular Mechanics, Inc., 1953.

Corbin, T. J. *Block Printing on Fabrics.* New York, N. Y.: Pitman Publishing Co., 1934.

Denny, G. G. *Fabrics 6th Edition Revised.* Philadelphia, Pa.: J. B. Lippincott Co., 1947.

Dobson, M. S. *Black Printing and Cutting by Hand from Wood, Linoleum and Other Media.* New York, N. Y.: Pitman Publishing Co., 1930.

Eckgren and Fishel. *500 Line Ideas for the Grade Teacher.* Chicago, Ill.: Row Peterson,Co., 1952.

Fearing, Kelly, *et al.* *Our Expanding Vision Book 7.* Austin, Tex.: W. S. Benson Co., 1960.

Flam, Davis S. *Art Decorations.* New York, N. Y.: Homecraft, 1950.

Frankenfield, Henry. *Block Printing with Linoleum.* Camden, N. J.: C. Howard Hunt and Co., 1940.

Hayter, S. W. *About Prints.* New York, N. Y.: Oxford University Press, 1962.

Heller, Jules. *Printmaking Today.* New York, N. Y.: Holt, Rinehart and Winston, 1958.

Other:

BASKETRY

Maginley, C. J. *Children's Activities.* "A May Basket to Weave", May, 1957.

Maris, Irena. *Holiday Arts.* New York, N. Y.: Owen Publishing Co., 1959.

Other:

CERAMICS AND POTTERY

Association for Childhood Ed. Int. *Creating with Materials for Work and Play.* (Bulletin No. 5) Washington 16, D. C.: 1957.

Ball, F. Carlton and Janice Lovoos. *Making Pottery Without a Wheel.* New York, N. Y.: Reinhold Publishing Corp.

Bell, M. G. *Practical Ceramics.* Montclair, N. J.: Bell Ceramics, Inc. Ceramics Monthly, Columbus, Ohio.

Drake, Kenneth. *Simple Pottery.* London, Studio Vista; New York, N. Y.: Watson–Guptill, 1966.

Duncan, Julia Hamlin. *How to Make Pottery and Ceramic Sculpture.* Garden City, N. Y.: Doubleday, 1960.

Fearing, Kelly. *Our Expanding Vision.* Austin, Tex.: W. S. Benson Co., 1960.
Fiore, R. R. *Fundamentals of Clay Modeling.* House of Little Books, 1946.
Foley, Doris E. *Art Recipes.* Dansville, N. Y.: Owen Publishing Co., 1960.
Home, Ruth M. *Ceramics for the Potter.* Brooklyn, N. Y.: Bennet, Rebecca Publishing, Inc., 1953.
Janeway, Carol. *Ceramics and Pottery Making for Everyone.* New York, N. Y.: Tudor Publishing Co., 1950.
Kellogg, A. M. *How To Teach Clay Modeling.* Chicago, Ill.: Flanagan, 1930.
Kelly and Roukes. *Let's Make A Mural.* San Francisco, Calif.: Fearon Publishing Co., 1959.
Kenny, John B. *Ceramic Design.* Philadelphia, Pa.: Chilton Book Co., 1963.
________. *The Complete Book of Pottery.* Philadelphia, Pa.: Chilton Book Co., 1949.
Kenny, J. B. *The Complete Book of Pottery Making.* New York, N. Y.: Greenberg Publishing Co., Inc., 1959.
Krum, Josephine R. *Hand-Built Pottery.* Scranton, Pa.: International Textbook Co., 1960.
Leach, Bernard. *A Potters Book.* New York, N. Y.: Transatlantic Arts, Inc., 1948.
Lembach, John. *Modeling Clay in the Dark.* Worcester, Mass.: School Arts Magazine, October, 1957.
Lemming, John. *Fun With Clay.* Philadelphia, Pa.: J. B. Lippincott Co., 1944.
Maris, Irena. *Holiday Art.* Dansville, N. Y.: F. A. Owen Publishing Co., 1959.
Marxhausen, Richard. *Clay.* Worcester, Mass.: School Arts Magazine, October, 1957.
Nelson, Glen C. *Ceramics.* New York, N. Y.: Holt, Rinehart and Winston, 1960.
Norton, F.H. *Ceramics for the Artist Potter.* Reading, Mass.: Addison-Wesley Publishing Co., Inc., 1956.
Parmelee, Cullen Warren. *Ceramic Glazes.* Cahners Publishing Co., 1951.
Poor, H. V. *A Book of Pottery: From Mud Into Immortality.* New York, N. Y.: Prentice-Hall, Inc.
Randall, R. H. *Ceramics Sculpture.* New York, N. Y.: Watson-Guptill, 1948.
Rhodes, Daniel. *Clay and Glazes for the Potter.* Philadelphia, Pa.: Chilton Book Co., 1957.
School Arts. *Creative Hands Bookshop.* Worchester, Mass.
Shore, Frank. *Pictures With Clay.* Worcester, Mass.: School Arts Magazine, February, 1959.
Snead, Jane. *Potter's Primer.* Philadelphia, Pa.: Ceramics Studio.
State Department of Education. *Art Materials and Formulas.* (Bulletins No. 3 and 9) Madison, Wis.: 1960.
Stewart. *Ceramics For All.* New York, N. Y.: Barnes and Noble, Inc.
Studio 31. *Ceramics.* Glenville, Conn.: Ettly Studios, Inc.
Thompson, Seely. *Activities in Ceramics.* Bloomington, Ill.: McKnight and McKnight Publishing Co., 1956.
Trevor, Henry. *Pottery Step By Step.* New York, N. Y.: Watson-Guptill Publishing Co., 1966.
Wheeler, I. W. *Playing With Clay.* New York, N. Y.: Macmillan Co., 1935.
Wolfe, Jack D. *Ceramics, Sculpture, and Enamelling.* Brooklyn, N. Y.
Other:

COPPER ENAMELLING

Baxter, W. T. *Jewelry, Gem Cutting and Metalcraft.* New York, N. Y.: McGraw-Hill Co., 1950.
Connors, Dorothy. *Gadgets Galore.* Chicago, Ill.: Popular Mechanics Co., 1953.
Dragunas, Andrew. *Creating Jewelry for Fun and Profit.* New York, N. Y.: Harper and Row Publishers, 1947.
Eckgren and Fishel. *500 Line Ideas for the Grade Teacher.* Chicago, Ill.: Row Peterson, Co., 1960.
Feirer, John L. *Modern Metalcraft.* Peoria, Ill.: Charles A. Bennett Co., 1965.
Handcrafters, The. *Metal Modeling Handicraft.* Waupun, Wis.: 1938.

Mazoni, Peter. *Metalcraft for Amateurs.* Boston, Mass.: The Beacon Press, 1935.
Modern. *American Trinkit.* Chicago, Ill.: 1960.
Pack, Greta. *Jewelry and Enamelling.* New York, N. Y.: D. Von Nostrand Co., 1948.
Pauly, A. *Copper Tooling.* "Pacific Arts and Crafts" Inglewood, Calif.: 1948.
Payne, A. F. *Art Metalwork.* Peoria, Ill.: Charles A. Bennett Co.
Peterson, L. C. *101 Metal-Working Projects.* Milwaukee, Wis.: Bruce Publishing Co., 1929.
Scharff, Robert. *Handicraft Hobbies for Profit.* New York, N. Y.: McGraw-Hill Co., 1952.
Smith, F. R. *Small Jewelry.* New York, N. Y.: Pitman Publishing Co., 1931.
Thomas, Richard. *Metalsmithing for the Artist-Craftsman.* Philadelphia, Pa.: Chilton Book Co., 1960.
Von Neumann, Robert. *The Design and Creation of Jewelry.* Philadelphia, Pa.: Chilton Book Co., 1961.
Wiener, Louis. *Hand Made Jewelry.* New York, N. Y.: D. Van Nostrand Co., 1960.
Winebrenner, Kenneth D. *Jewelry Making.* Scranton, Pa.: Informational Textbook Co.
Winson, H. *Silverwork and Jewelry.* New York, N. Y.: Appleton Co.
Other:

LEATHER

Aller, Doris. *Sunset Leather Craft Book.* Menlo Park, Calif.: Lane Publishing Co., 1952.
Baird, F. O. *Leather Secrets.* Manitou Springs, Colo.: F. O. Baird, 1951.
Cherry, Raymond. *General Leathercraft.* Bloomington, Ill.: McKnight and McKnight Publishing Co., 1955.
Christopher, F. J. and Eva Clarke. *Leather Work.* New York, N. Y.: Dover Publications, Inc., 1952.
Cramlet, Ross C. *Fundamentals of Leathercraft.* Milwaukee, Wis.: The Bruce Publishing Co., 1939.
Dean, John W. *Leathercraft Techniques and Designs.* Bloomington, Ill.: McKnight and McKnight Publishing Co., 1950.
Dougherty, Betty. *Your Leatherwork.* Peoria, Ill.: Charles A. Bennett Co., Inc., 1947.
Grant, Bruce. *Leather Braiding.* Cambridge, Md.: Cornell Maritime Press, 1950.
Griffin, Ken. *Ken Griffin's Scrap Book.* Los Angeles, Calif.: Craftool Company, 1952.
Griswold, Lester. *Leatherwork.* New Brunswick, N. J.: Boy Scouts of American National Council, 1951.
Groneman, Chris H. *Leather Tooling and Carving.* Scranton, Pa.: Laurel Publishers, 1951.
Johnson, L. *Leatherwork.* London, England: C. Arthur Pearson, Ltd., 1949.
Johnson, William H. and Louis V. Newkirk. *Leathercraft.* St. Paul, Minn.: Webb Publishing Co., 1945.
Leatherwork Industries of America. *Dictionary of Leather Terminology.* New York, N. Y.: Leather Industries of Amercia, 1946.
Mannel, Elise. *Leathercraft Is Fun.* Milwaukee, Wis.: The Bruce Publishing Company, 1952.
Stohlman, Al. *How to Carve Leather.* Los Angeles, Calif.: Craftool Company, 1952.
Thompson, Robert L. *Leathercraft.* New York, N. Y.: D. Van Nostrand Co., Inc., 1947.
Waterer, John W. *Leather and Craftsmanship.* London, England: Faber and Faber Ltd., 1950.
Woolf, Natalie. *Glove Making for Beginners.* Bloomington, Ill.: McKnight and McKnight Publishing Co., 1951.
Other:

MOSAICS

Aller, Doris and Diane Lee. *Sunset Mosaics.* Menlo Park, Calif.: Lane Publishing Co., 1959.
Argiro, Larry. *Mosaic Art Today.* Scranton, Pa.: International Textbook Co., 1961.
Art Education. *Journal of Art Education Association.* New York, N. Y.: Columbia University, 1959.
Arts and Crafts. College Park, Md.: Distributors, Inc.
Ceramics Monthly. Columbus, Ohio.
Immaculate Heart College. Art Department, Los Angeles, Calif.: 1958.
Kelly and Roukes. *Let's Make A Mural.* San Francisco, Calif.: Fearon Publishing Co., 1959.
Maris, Irena. *Paper Art.* Dansville, N. Y.: Owen Publishing Co., 1960.
Mary, Sister Magdalen, I. H. M. *Mosaics and Colleges: Mosaics for Everyone.* $3.00. Immaculate Heart College: 5515 Franklin Ave., Los Angeles, Calif.
Other:

PAPER

Amon, Martha and Ruth Rawson. *Handicraft Simplified.* Bloomington, Ill.: McKnight and McKnight Publishing Co., 1961.
Associations for Childhood Ed. Int. *Creating with Materials for Work and Play.* (Bulletin Number 5) Washington, D. C., 1957.
Baranski, Matthew. *Mask Making.* Worchester, Mass.: Davis Publications, Inc., 1955.
Becker, Edith C. *Adventures with Scissors and Paper.* Scranton, Pa.: International Textbook Co., 1959.
Betts, Victoria Bedford. *Exploring Papier Mache.* Worchester, Mass.: Davis Publications, Inc., 1955.
Connors, Dorothy. *Gadgets Galore.* Chicago, Ill.: Popular Mechanics, Inc., 1953.
Eckgren and Fishel. *500 Line Ideas for the Grade Teacher.* Chicago, Ill.: Row Peterson Co., 1960.
Foley, Doris E. *Art Recipes.* Instructor Handbook Series, Dansville, N. Y.: F. A. Owen Publishing Co., 1960.
Johnson, Lillian. *Papier Mache.* New York, N. Y.: David McKay Co., Inc., 1959.
Johnson, Mary Grace. *Paper Sculpture.* Worchester, Mass.: Davis Publications, Inc., 1959.
Johnson, Paulson. *Creating With Paper.* Seattle, Wash.: University of Washington Press.
Kelley and Roukes. *Let's Make A Mural.* San Francisco, Calif.: Fearon Publishing Co., 1959.
Lord, Lois. *College and Construction in Elementary and Junior High Schools.* Worchester, Mass.: Davis Publications, Inc., 1958.
Maris, Irena. *Holiday Art.* Dansville, N. Y.: F. A. Owen Publishing Co., 1959.
__________. *Holiday Fun.* Dansville, N. Y.: F. A. Owen Publishing Co., 1959.
__________. *Paper Art.* Dansville, N. Y.: F. A. Owen Publishing Co., 1960.
Miller, J. V. *Paper Sculpture and Construction.* Peoria, Ill.: Charles A. Bennett Co., 1957.
Morgan, Natalie. *Handicraft.* Grosset Co., 1947.
"Paper as a Creative Art Medium". *School Arts.* Worchester, Mass.: December, 1957.
Pauli, Anna and Margaret Mitzit. *Paper Figures.* Peoria, Ill.: Charles A. Bennett Co.
Rottger, Ernst. *Creative Paper Design.* New York, N. Y.: Reinhold Publishing Corp., 1961.
Other:

PLASTICS

Bass, Stephen. *Plastics and You.* New York, N.Y.: Eastwood–Steli Company, 1947.
Cook, James G. *The Miracle of Plastics.* New York, N.Y.: Dial Press, 1964.
Cope, Dwight. *Plastics Book.* Chicago: Goodheart–Wilcox Co., 1957.
DuBois, John H. *Plastics.* New York, N.Y.: Reinhold Publishing Corp., 1967.
Hooper, Rodney. *Plastics for the Home Craftsman.* J. B. Lippincott Co., 1953.
Newman, Thelma. *Plastics as an Art Form.* Philadelphia: Chilton Books, 1964.
Simonds, Herbert. *A Concise Guide to Plastics.* 2nd Edition, 1963.
Spielman, Patrick. *Modern Projects in Wood, Metal and Plastics.* Milwaukee: Bruce Publishing Co., 1964.
Wolfe, Bernard. *Plastics; What Everyone Should Know.* Bobbs, 1945.
Other:

WEAVING

Albers, Anni. *On Weaving.* Middleton, Conn.: Wesleyan University Press, 1965.
Alexander, Marthann. *Weaving Handcraft.* Bloomington, Ill.: McKnight and McKnight Publishing Co., 1958.
Allen, Edith Louise. *Weaving You Can Do.* Peoria, Ill.: Manual Arts Press.
Atwater, M. M. *The Shuttle-Craft Book of American Handweaving.* New York, N. Y.: Macmillan Co., 1951.
Beriau, Oscar. *Home Weaving.* Gardenvale, Quebec, Canada: Arts and Crafts of Gardenvale, Inc., 1947.
Black, Mary E. *Key To Weaving.* Milwaukee, Wis.: The Bruce Publishing Co.
Davison, M. P. *A Handweaver's Pattern Book.* Swarthmore, Pa.: (revised edition) 1951.
Karasz, Mariska. *Adventure in Stitches.* New York, N. Y.: McGraw-Hill Book Co., 1942.
Mochrie, Elsie. *Simple Weaving with Patterns and Suggestions For Its Use.* (3rd Edition) Leicester, England: Dryad Press, 1934.
Overman, Ruth and Lula Smith. *Contemporary Handweaving.* The Iowa State College Press, Ames, Iowa.
Rainey, Sarita R. *Weaving Without A Loom.* Daris Publications, 1966.
Tait, Lou. *Weaving at the Little Loom House.* Louisville, Ky.: Lou Tait.
Van Dommelen, D. B. *Decorative Wall Hangings.* Art With Fabric. New York, N. Y.: Funk and Wagnalls Co., 1962.
Worst, Edward F. *Foot-Power Loom Weaving.* Milwaukee, Wis.: Bruce Publishing Co.
Other:

WOOD

Aller, Doris. *Sunset Wood Carving Book.* Menlo Park, Calif.: Lane Publishing Co., 1951.
Association for Childhood Ed. Int. *Creating With Materials for Work and Play.* (Bulletin No. 5) Washington, D. C.: 1957.
Bassett, Kendall T. and Arthur B. Thurman. *How To Make Objects With Wood.* New York, N. Y.: The Museum of Modern Art, 1951.

Briggs, John R. *Crafts of Woodcuts.* Sterling, 1963.
Dank, M. C. *Creative Crafts in Wood.* Peoria, Ill.: Charles A. Bennett.
Foley, Doris E. *Art Recipes.* Instructor Handbook Series. Dansville, N. Y.: F. A. Owen Publishing Co., 1960.
Gross, Chaim. *Technique of Wood Sculpture.* Arco, 1964.
Handbook for Art Education in the Elementary School. *Wood-Carving.* Eau Claire, Wis.
Hunt, Ben. *Whittling Book.* Milwaukee, Wis.: Bruce Publishing Co.
Mankin, Victor J. *Modernistic Chip Carving.* Milwaukee, Wis.: Bruce Publishing Co., 1953.
Maris, Irena. *Paper Art Toothpicks.* Dansville, N. Y.: F. A. Owen Publishing Co., 1960.
Moore, H. *Chip Carving.* Peoria, Ill.: Charles A. Bennett Co.
Newkirk, L. V. and L. Zutter. *Crafts for Everyone.* Vol. 1, Scranton, Pa.: International Textbook Co., 1951.
__________. *Your Craft Book.* Princeton, N. J.: D. Van Norstrand Co., Inc., 1955.
Pitman Publishing Company, New York, N. Y.: *Handicraft Woodwork.*
Rood, John. *Sculpture in Wood.* Minneapolis, Minn.: University of Minnesota Press, 1950.
Rothenstein, Michael. *Linocuts and Woodcuts.* Sterling, 1963.
Scharff, Robert. *Handicraft Hobbies for Profit.* New York, N. Y.: McGraw-Hill Book Co., 1952.
Tangerman, E. J. *Design and Figure Carving.* New York, N. Y.: McGraw-Hill Book Co., 1940.
__________. *Whittling and Wood Carving.* New York, N. Y.: McGraw-Hill Book Co., 1940.
Waltner, Elma. *Carving Animal Caricatures.* Bloomington, Ill.: McKnight and McKnight Publishing Co., 1951.
X-Acto Crescent Products Company. *Whittling Is Easy.* New York, N. Y.
Other:

DESIGN

Anderson, D. *Elements of Design.* New York, N. Y.: Holt, Rinehart and Winston, Inc., 1961.
Baldinger, Wallace S. *The Visual Arts.* New York, N. Y.: Holt, Rinehart and Winston, Inc., 1960.
Benlin, Marjorie R. *Design Through Discovery.* New York, N.Y.: Holt, Rinehart and Winston, Inc., 1963.
Collier, Graham. *Form Space and Vision.* New York, N. Y.: Prentice-Hall, Inc., 1963.
Downer, Marion. *Story of Design.* New York, N.Y.: Lothrop, 1963, Lee and Shephard Co.
Gabo, Naum. *Of Diverse Arts.* The A. W. Mellon Lectures in the Fine Art delivered at the National Gallery of Art, Washington, D. C. New York, N. Y.: Bollinger Foundation, 1962.
Garrett, L. *Visual Design: A Problem Solving Approach.* New York, N. Y.: Reinhold Publishing,Corp., 1966.
Gropius, Walter, Herbert Bayer and Ilse Gropius. Bauhaus: 1919–1928, *Museum of Modern Art.* New York, N. Y.: 1939.
Kepes, Gyorgy. *Language of Vision.* Chicago, Ill.: Paul Theobald, 1945.
Moseley, S., P. Johnson and H. Koenig. *Crafts Design.* Belmont, Calif.: Wadsworth Publishing Co., Inc.
Other:

INDEX